COASTLINE ELDERLY SERVICES, INC.

This cookbook is a collection of prize-winning recipes
from 25 years of the Standard-Times' Cooking Contest,
Coastline Elderly Services, Inc., and individuals;
they are not necessarily original recipes.
This first edition is to celebrate the Standard-Times' 25th
anniversary and Coastline's 20th anniversary.
Proceeds from the sale of this book
will go to benefit the Standard-Times'
Neediest Family Fund and Coastline's senior programs.

Copyright 1997 Coastline Elderly Services, Inc.
Published by Coastline Elderly Services, Inc.
1646 Purchase Street, New Bedford, MA 02740
(508) 999-6400

Designed, Edited and Manufactured by
Favorite Recipes® Press
an imprint of

FRP

P.O. Box 305142, Nashville, TN 37230
1-800-358-0560

Book Design by Brad Whitfield and Susan Breining

ISBN: 0-9657182-0-4
Library of Congress Catalog Number: 97-66396

Manufactured in the United States of America
First Printing: 1997
5,000 copies

Cover Art and Illustrations by Derek Lavoie

Table of Contents

This book is dedicated to all the people
who have provided their knowledge and wisdom
to allow Coastline Elderly Services, Inc.,
the opportunity to provide care
to the Greater New Bedford area
and surrounding communities
for the past twenty years.

Acknowledgements

We wish to express our sincere appreciation
to the following organizations and individuals
for their assistance in the publishing of this book:

Maria Connor

Lucille Emin

Ann McCrillis

Evelyn Pursley

Karen Samson

Georgette Simon

Charles N. Sisson

The Standard-Times

Nancy Wheeler

RESTAURANT CONTRIBUTORS

Blue Point Restaurant

Fairhaven Chowder House

Freestone's City Grill

Mattapoisett Inn

Riccardi's

The Pasta House

Worden's

Foreword

The Standard-Times Newspaper Cookbook and Recipe Contest
was established in the 1970s by then-Lifestyles editor Jonathan Miller.
Down through the years, the categories have changed to reflect trends:
contestants have dreamed up low-cal dishes, pasta recipes,
and, in tough times, budget entrées.
Sometimes an ingredient is the star,
such as peanut butter, mushrooms, poultry, or fruit.
Ethnic cookery, seafood, and fancy desserts have been mainstay categories.
In 1996, more than 280 entries were submitted by hopeful contestants—
with a growing number of men among them.
A judges' panel composed of food professionals, led for many years
by Evelyn Pursley, participates in the taste-off,
held in recent years at the vocational school as a featured attraction
of the Greater New Bedford Home Show in early March.
At the taste-off, the winners of seven categories vie for first-, second-,
and third-place awards, as well as for the grand prize,
which for a number of years has been $500 in cash.
But perhaps the most valuable "prize" awarded in the annual recipe contest
is the warm camaraderie among the competing chefs,
reflecting that of all cooks who love the culinary arts.

Joanna McQuillan Weeks
Standard-Times Food Editor

Preface

On behalf of everyone associated with Coastline Elderly Services, Inc.,
we wish to thank you for supporting our agency for our first twenty years.
We have always worked to be the very best we could be and to develop
a range of services that meet the unique needs of our community.
It is especially gratifying that we have been able to team up
with the Standard-Times as they celebrate their twenty-fifth anniversary
of the cooking contest and the Neediest Family Fund.
The proceeds of this cookbook will go to assist our most vulnerable citizens,
our children and our seniors.
When we started this project, we decided that we wanted it
to be something truly different, representative of the area
we have come to know as the SouthCoast.
We chose lighthouses because they are
both landmarks in our area and a beacon of hope in a sea of change.
We also chose some of New Bedford's finest restaurants to represent the
outstanding culinary standards in our area, while highlighting
the efforts of our area's best chefs over the past twenty-five years.
I feel we have accomplished this and made available to you a cookbook
that is second to none and is truly representative of our area.
Thank you for supporting us by purchasing this book and for your continued support
for us and the newspaper cooking contests on into the next century.

Yours truly,
Charlie Sisson
Executive Director, Coastline Elderly Services, Inc.

Introduction

"Lighthouses dot the sea shore on every coast.
Their quiet reverent beauty brings to mind visions of stormy seas,
ships in distress, shipwrecks and sunken treasures strewn across the ocean floor.
Their beacons are like solitary soldiers sent to guard the lives
and precious cargo of those who dare to challenge an unforgiving sea.
A beacon to show the way, give hope and bring all safely home."

Once known as the "Whaling Capital of the World,"
the city of New Bedford has relied on the bounty of the sea for its prosperity.
Whaling started in 1765; by 1857 over 328 whaling vessels
took sail from New Bedford harbor. Lighthouses built in the 1790s
made this growth possible by guiding the ships with their precious cargo
of whale oil and men safely into port and home to the loved ones
who waited for their return. As the whaling days dwindled away,
the fishing industry and mercantile shipping provided new growth for the area.
While textiles also played a major role in that growth,
it was the sea and its bounty that brought the diverse cultural heritage
that is New Bedford today.

Karen Samson

Hors d'Oeuvres

New Bedford Lightship

Lightships served as floating lighthouses anchored near dangerous water where building a lighthouse was impractical or impossible. Coast Guardsmen stayed at their posts regardless of the weather to guide other vessels through fog, storms, and even hurricanes.

The New Bedford Lightship was built in 1930 and is now on display by the Coast Guard in New Bedford.

CHICKEN AND SHRIMP EGG ROLLS

6 ounces shrimp, peeled, cooked, deveined
1 large onion, finely chopped
2 cloves of garlic, minced
1 teaspoon vegetable oil
2 cups shredded Chinese cabbage
1 (10-ounce) can bean sprouts
1 cup sliced mushrooms
1½ cups chopped cooked chicken
1 egg, lightly beaten
2 teaspoons soy sauce
⅛ teaspoon cayenne
8 egg roll wrappers
4 teaspoons vegetable oil

Chop the shrimp and set aside. Sauté the onion and garlic in 1 teaspoon oil in a wok or large skillet for 3 minutes or until tender. Add the cabbage, bean sprouts and mushrooms. Sauté for 3 minutes. Combine the cabbage mixture, shrimp, chicken, egg, soy sauce and cayenne in a large bowl and mix well. Spoon ½ cup of the chicken filling down the center of an egg roll wrapper. Fold 1 long side of the wrapper over the top and around the filling. Fold in both ends, compressing the mixture into the wrapper. Fold the remaining long side up and over the top and ends. Brush with ½ teaspoon of the 4 teaspoons oil. Repeat with the remaining chicken filling and egg roll wrappers. Place the filled wrappers seam side down on a large baking sheet. Bake at 350 degrees for 25 minutes or until golden brown. Note: Egg roll wrappers can be found in the produce section or refrigerated section of the supermarket.

Yield: 8 servings

Lauren A. Cohen

Golden Chicken Nuggets

2 chicken breasts, boned, skinned
1/3 cup dry bread crumbs
1/4 cup grated Parmesan cheese
3/4 teaspoon salt

1/4 teaspoon pepper
1/2 teaspoon thyme
1 teaspoon basil
1/3 cup melted butter

Rinse the chicken and pat dry. Cut into 1-inch pieces. Mix the bread crumbs, cheese, salt, pepper, thyme and basil in a bowl. Dip the chicken pieces in the butter. Roll in the herb mixture. Arrange in a single layer in a foil-lined baking pan. Bake at 425 degrees for 10 to 12 minutes or until golden brown; do not overbake. Serve hot.

Yield: 12 to 16 servings

Donna Cordeira

Marinated Chicken Wings

2 to 3 pounds chicken wings
1/2 cup soy sauce
1 cup Italian salad dressing
2 cups orange juice

1 1/4 cups maple syrup
1 cup vegetable oil
1 cup packed brown sugar
6 to 8 cloves of garlic, pressed

Rinse the chicken and pat dry. Combine the soy sauce, salad dressing, orange juice, syrup, oil, brown sugar and garlic in a 10-quart or larger kettle and mix well. Add the chicken. Marinate in the refrigerator for 24 to 48 hours, stirring frequently. Remove the chicken from the marinade; discard the marinade. Arrange the chicken in a single layer in a shallow baking pan. Do not allow the pieces to touch. Bake, covered with foil, at 350 degrees for 1 hour. Bake, uncovered, for 30 minutes or until the chicken is brown. Note: The chicken wings may be cut at the joint to allow for ease in handling and eating.

Yield: 15 servings

Terri Canty

CHILES RELLENOS

½ cup butter
½ cup flour
½ teaspoon salt
1 teaspoon baking powder
10 eggs, lightly beaten

16 ounces cottage cheese
1 pound Monterey Jack cheese,
  shredded
1 (4-ounce) can chopped
  green chiles

Melt the butter in a 9x13-inch baking dish. Combine the butter, flour, salt, baking powder, eggs, cottage cheese, Monterey Jack cheese and green chiles in a bowl and mix well. Pour into the baking dish. Bake at 350 degrees for 35 to 40 minutes or until heated through. Cool slightly. Cut into small squares.

Yield: 3 dozen

Nancy Swanson

QUICK CRAB MEAT HORS D'OEUVRES

6 English muffins, split into halves
1 jar Old English cheese
1 tablespoon butter
⅛ teaspoon crushed garlic
  or garlic salt

1 tablespoon mayonnaise
1 (6-ounce) can crab meat, drained

Arrange the muffin halves on a baking sheet. Blend the cheese, butter, garlic and mayonnaise in a medium mixer bowl. Stir in the crab meat. Spread on the muffin halves. Freeze for 30 minutes or until firm. Cut each muffin into 4 pieces. Store in a covered plastic container until needed. Place desired number of pieces on a rack in a broiler pan. Broil for 5 minutes or until light brown. Serve hot.

Yield: 4 dozen

Barbara Johansen

Vegetarian Eggplant Meatballs

3 cloves of garlic, minced
3 tablespoons olive oil
1 large eggplant, peeled, diced
1 teaspoon water
1 to 1½ cups seasoned
bread crumbs

½ cup chopped fresh parsley
2 eggs, beaten
½ cup shredded Cheddar cheese
Vegetable oil

Sauté the garlic in the olive oil in a large saucepan. Add the eggplant and water. Cook, covered, over low heat until the eggplant is very tender. Cool slightly. Mix the bread crumbs, parsley, eggs and cheese in a large bowl. Add the eggplant and mix well. Let stand for 20 to 30 minutes or until cool enough to handle. Shape the mixture into balls. The meatballs may be browned on all sides in vegetable oil or oven-baked at 325 degrees for 30 minutes. Stir into spaghetti sauce or serve as an appetizer with marinara sauce.

Yield: 12 to 16 servings

Tina Gaudette

Cape Cod Peanuts

24 hard-shell clams (small quahogs)
¾ cup melted butter or margarine
1½ cups very fine bread crumbs
2 tablespoons brown sugar
2 tablespoons grated
Parmesan cheese

3 tablespoons finely chopped
green bell pepper
1 teaspoon oregano
¼ teaspoon salt
⅛ teaspoon pepper
24 (1-inch) squares bacon

Open and drain the clams, reserving the liquid. Mix the butter, bread crumbs, brown sugar, cheese, green pepper, oregano, salt and pepper in a bowl. Place the clams on a baking sheet. Spoon the cheese mixture onto the clams. Drizzle the reserved liquid over the clams. Top each with a bacon square. Bake at 375 degrees for 15 minutes. Serve immediately. Note: If the bacon is not crisp at the end of the baking time, broil for 1 minute or until crisp.

Yield: 6 servings

Theresa Francoeur

SPINACH CHEESE BITES

1 (10-ounce) package sliced pepperoni
1 (10-ounce) package frozen chopped spinach, thawed, drained
2 cups ricotta cheese
1½ cups freshly grated Parmesan cheese
1⅓ cups finely chopped fresh mushrooms
¼ cup finely chopped onion
1 teaspoon dried oregano
½ teaspoon salt
2 eggs, lightly beaten
¼ cup sour cream

Lightly grease 4 miniature muffin pans. Place 1 pepperoni slice in each of 12 individual muffin cups in each pan. Cut the remaining pepperoni slices into wedges and set aside. Combine the spinach, ricotta cheese, Parmesan cheese, mushrooms, onion, oregano, salt and eggs in a bowl and mix well. Spoon into the muffin cups. Bake at 375 degrees for 20 to 25 minutes or until light brown. Cool for 10 minutes. Remove gently to a serving plate. Top each with a dollop of sour cream and a pepperoni wedge. Serve warm. Note: May be baked and stored in the freezer for up to 3 months. To serve, thaw in the refrigerator. Bake at 350 degrees for 10 minutes or until heated through. Top with sour cream and pepperoni wedges.

Yield: 4 dozen

Rhonda Arno

Pepper Swiss Cheese Ball

6 ounces cream cheese, softened
½ cup sour cream
¼ teaspoon garlic salt
1½ cups shredded Swiss cheese

2 tablespoons chopped
fresh parsley
2 to 3 tablespoons coarsely
ground pepper

Beat the cream cheese in a mixer bowl at medium speed for 1 to 2 minutes or until smooth, scraping the bowl frequently. Add the sour cream and garlic salt and beat until mixed. Stir in the cheese and parsley. Chill for 2 hours or longer. Shape into a ball or log. Roll in the pepper to coat. Chill until serving time.

Yield: 16 to 20 servings

Dorothy E. Oliviera

Mock Boursin

8 ounces whipped unsalted
butter, softened
12 ounces cream cheese, softened
¼ teaspoon garlic powder
¼ teaspoon salt
1 teaspoon oregano

¼ teaspoon thyme
¼ teaspoon marjoram
¼ teaspoon dill
¼ teaspoon pepper
¼ teaspoon basil

Mash the butter and cream cheese with a fork in a bowl. Add the garlic powder and salt and mix well. Add the oregano, thyme, marjoram, dill, pepper and basil and mix well. Shape into a ball and place in a bowl. Chill thoroughly. Invert onto a plate. Garnish with parsley and surround with crackers. Serve at room temperature.

Yield: 20 to 30 servings

Mrs. Paul Buffam

HOT PEPPER DIP

2 small hot peppers, seeded,
finely chopped
8 ounces cottage cheese

½ cup yogurt
1 tablespoon vinegar
1 large green or red bell pepper

Combine the hot peppers and cottage cheese in a food processor container or blender container. Process until smooth. Stir in the yogurt and vinegar. Chill for 2 hours or longer to blend the flavors. Slice off the top of the green pepper and remove the seeds. Pour in the dip. Place the green pepper in the center of a serving platter. Surround with bite-size cold fresh vegetables.

Yield: 1¾ cups

Beverly Tavares

SHRIMP COCKTAIL SAUCE

½ cup horseradish
1 cup chili sauce
1 cup catsup
Salt and pepper to taste

⅛ teaspoon sugar, or to taste
1 teaspoon olive oil
Juice of 2 lemons
2 teaspoons Worcestershire sauce

Mix the horseradish, chili sauce, catsup, salt, pepper, sugar and olive oil in a bowl. Add the lemon juice and Worcestershire sauce and mix well. Chill for 30 minutes or longer. Serve over shrimp or seafood or as a dip for boiled, fried or barbecued shrimp or ribs.

Yield: 2½ to 3 cups

Mrs. N. E. Wright

SHRIMP SPREAD

3 ounces cream cheese, softened
½ (10-ounce) can tomato soup
2 (4-ounce) cans small
  shrimp, mashed
1 envelope unflavored gelatin

¾ cup mayonnaise
½ cup chopped celery
¼ cup chopped onion
½ teaspoon salt

Mix the cream cheese and soup in a large bowl. Add the shrimp and mix well. Soften the gelatin in a small amount of cold water in a saucepan. Heat until the gelatin is dissolved. Add the gelatin, mayonnaise, celery, onion and salt to the shrimp mixture and mix well. Pour into a greased mold. Chill until set. Spread over crackers.
Yield: 3 to 4 cups

Mrs. Arthur Lafrenais

MEXICAN DELIGHT DIP

8 ounces cream cheese, softened
1 (3-ounce) can jalapeño peppers
1 (15-ounce) can hot chili

3½ ounces Cheddar cheese or
Monterey Jack cheese, shredded

Layer the cream cheese, jalapeños, chili and cheese in a glass baking dish in the order listed. Bake at 375 degrees until bubbly. Serve with nacho chips.
Yield: 6 servings

Barbara Stevens

PORTUGUESE FAVAS

3 onions, chopped
½ cup olive oil
1½ cups catsup
½ cup water
¼ cup parsley
1 teaspoon salt
1 teaspoon crushed red pepper
4 cans fava beans, drained

Brown the onions in the olive oil in a 9-inch skillet; drain well. Combine the onions,
catsup, water, parsley, salt and red pepper in the skillet and mix well. Simmer for 20 minutes.
Place the fava beans in a 4-quart saucepan. Pour the onion mixture over the beans.
Bring to a boil. Simmer for 20 minutes. Serve immediately.
Yield: 8 servings

John Murray

*Soups &
Salads*

Palmer Island Lighthouse

Located in New Bedford Harbor, Palmer Island Lighthouse was built in *1849* and served until *1941* when its light was automated and transferred to Butler Flats Lighthouse.

A hurricane destroyed the keeper's house in *1938*. During this storm the keeper was injured and his wife was drowned as they attempted to reach the light.

Black Bean Soup

1 pound black beans
¼ cup vegetable oil
2 teaspoons cumin seeds
2 teaspoons mustard seeds
4 to 6 cloves of garlic, crushed
3 to 4 hot chile peppers, seeded, chopped (optional)
3 medium onions, diced
2 large cans crushed tomatoes
2 tablespoons dried mint
2 tablespoons dried basil
2 teaspoons salt
3 tablespoons dark miso (see Note)
Chopped celery, potatoes, carrots, mushrooms, broccoli, cauliflower

Rinse and sort the beans. Combine with water to cover in a large pan and soak overnight; drain. Heat the oil in a 5-quart saucepan. Add the cumin seeds and mustard seeds. Cook until the seeds have stopped popping. Add the garlic and peppers. Sauté for 45 seconds or less. Add the onions. Sauté for 5 to 7 minutes or until tender. Add the beans, tomatoes and enough water to cover the beans. Bring to a boil. Simmer for 20 to 30 minutes. Add the mint, basil, salt, miso and desired amount of chopped vegetables. Add enough water to cover all the ingredients. Simmer until the beans are tender-crisp. Remove 2 to 3 cups of the beans and a small amount of liquid from the soup. Pour into a blender container. Process until liquefied and return to the soup. Simmer until the beans are tender. Note: Dark miso (aged soybean paste) is available at natural food stores and Japanese markets.

Yield: 5 quarts

Carol Gupte

HEARTY CORN CHOWDER

6 to 8 slices bacon
1 medium onion, coarsely chopped
4 medium potatoes, cut into ½-inch cubes
2 (16-ounce) cans cream-style corn
2 cups milk
2 tablespoons butter or margarine
1 teaspoon salt
⅛ teaspoon pepper, or to taste

Cook the bacon and onion in a skillet until the bacon is crisp. Drain on paper towels. Crumble the bacon. Boil the potatoes in water to cover in a saucepan until tender. Drain, reserving 1 cup cooking liquid. Combine the corn, milk, potatoes, reserved cooking liquid, bacon, onion, butter, salt and pepper in a 3-quart saucepan. Cook over low heat until heated through. Yield: 4 to 5 large servings

Judy MacGregor

*Don't throw away leftover dinner salad.
Turn it into chilled soup by processing it with chicken broth
until smooth and creamy. Add half-and-half or sour cream
if desired and season to taste.*

CREAM OF MUSHROOM SOUP

8 ounces fresh mushrooms
1½ cups water
2 cups diced potatoes
1 (10-ounce) can cream of mushroom soup
1 small can Pennsylvania Dutch mushrooms, drained
Salt and pepper to taste
1 cup milk
Rye bread croutons (see Note)

Wipe the fresh mushrooms clean and cut into slices. Bring the water and fresh mushrooms to a boil in a 2-quart saucepan. Boil for 5 minutes. Remove the mushrooms and set aside. Add the potatoes to the hot cooking liquid. Cook until tender. Add the soup and mix well. Cook for 5 to 8 minutes, stirring constantly. Add all the mushrooms. Season with salt and pepper. Stir in the milk. Bring slowly to a boil. Simmer for 5 minutes. Note: To prepare the croutons, cube 3 to 4 slices of rye bread (preferably hard-crust Polish rye). Brown in a toaster oven.
Serve on top of the soup.
Yield: 4 servings

Jennie M. Jardin

MUSHROOM AND POTATO CHOWDER

½ cup chopped onion
¼ cup butter or margarine
2 tablespoons all-purpose flour
1 teaspoon salt
½ teaspoon pepper
3 cups water

1 pound fresh mushrooms, sliced
1 cup chopped celery
1 cup diced peeled potatoes
½ cup chopped carrot
1 cup light cream
¼ cup grated Parmesan cheese

Sauté the onion in the butter in a large saucepan until tender. Add the flour, salt and pepper. Cook until the flour is brown, stirring constantly. Add the water gradually, stirring constantly. Bring to a boil. Boil for 1 minute, stirring constantly. Add the mushrooms, celery, potatoes and carrot; reduce the heat. Simmer, covered, for 30 minutes or until the vegetables are tender. Add the cream and cheese.

Yield: 4 to 6 servings

Heidi Nunes

PEA SOUP

1 (1-pound) package green
split peas
1 ham bone
2 quarts water

2 large onions, sliced
3 carrots, peeled, sliced
2 ribs celery, sliced

Rinse and sort the peas. Combine the ham bone and water in a large roasting pan. Add the onions, carrots and celery. Bring to a boil. Add the peas. Cook over low heat for 1 to 1½ hours or until the peas are very tender, stirring occasionally to avoid scorching. Remove the ham bone. Return any bits of ham to the pan. Add additional water if needed to thin the soup. Serve with oyster crackers or buns.

Yield: 8 to 10 servings

Louise Benoit

CREAM OF SPINACH SOUP

1 medium onion, chopped
2 tablespoons melted butter
1 (10-ounce) package frozen spinach, thawed, drained
1 quart chicken stock
3 tablespoons butter
3 tablespoons flour
1/4 teaspoon white pepper
1/4 teaspoon Greek seasoning
1 cup half-and-half

Sauté the onion in the melted butter in a skillet. Add the spinach. Cook, covered, over high heat for 3 to 5 minutes or until wilted. Spoon the spinach into a blender container. Add 1 cup of the chicken stock. Purée until smooth; set aside. Melt 3 tablespoons butter in a Dutch oven. Add the flour, stirring until smooth. Cook for 1 minute. Add the remaining 3 cups chicken stock gradually. Cook over medium heat until thick and bubbly, stirring constantly. Add the spinach, pepper and seasoning; reduce the heat. Simmer, covered, for 5 minutes. Stir in the half-and-half. Cook until heated through.

Yield: 6 to 8 servings

Kelley Serpa

Vegetarian Chowder

4 cups sliced zucchini
½ cup chopped onion
⅓ cup butter or margarine
⅓ cup flour
2 tablespoons minced parsley
1 teaspoon crushed basil
1 teaspoon salt
⅛ teaspoon pepper

3 cups water
1 chicken bouillon cube
1 (10-ounce) can evaporated milk
1 (16-ounce) can tomatoes, or
3 fresh tomatoes, peeled, chopped
1 cup shredded Monterey Jack
cheese (optional)

Sauté the zucchini and onion in the butter in a large saucepan. Stir in the flour, parsley, basil, salt and pepper. Add the water gradually, stirring constantly. Add the bouillon cube, evaporated milk and tomatoes. Bring to a boil. Simmer for 10 to 15 minutes or until heated through. Stir in the cheese.

Yield: 6 to 8 servings

Lynne Brodeur

Fish and Vegetable Chowder

2 tablespoons butter
1 onion, chopped
¼ cup flour
2 cups chicken stock
3 potatoes, cubed
4 carrots, thinly sliced

2 ribs celery, thinly sliced
1 pound whitefish, cod or
haddock, cut into 1-inch pieces
1 bay leaf
1 cup milk
1 cup whipping cream

Heat the butter in a 3-quart saucepan. Add the onion. Cook until the onion is yellow and tender. Add the flour. Cook for 2 minutes, stirring constantly. Add the chicken stock gradually, stirring constantly. Add the potatoes, carrots and celery. Cook, covered, for 10 to 15 minutes or until almost tender. Add the fish and bay leaf. Simmer, covered, for 5 to 10 minutes or until the vegetables and fish are cooked through. Add the milk and cream. Cook until heated through. Remove the bay leaf before serving.

Yield: 6 to 8 servings

Susan Schwager

MARY LOU'S FISH CHOWDER

1½ pounds fresh cod fillets
4 cups boiling water
3 medium potatoes, cut into small pieces
2 medium quahogs
1 cup boiling water
1 (1x1½x2-inch) piece salt pork, cut into small pieces
1 medium onion, cut vertically into slivers
2 cans evaporated milk
Pepper to taste

Place the fish in a colander over 4 quarts boiling water in a 5-quart saucepan. Steam, covered, until the fish flakes easily. Remove the fish and colander from the saucepan and set aside. Add the potatoes to the remaining cooking liquid in the saucepan. Cook until tender. Turn off the heat and add the fish. Drop the quahogs into 1 cup boiling water in a small saucepan. Cook, covered, until the shells open. Remove the quahogs from the shells and chop finely. Add the quahogs and their cooking liquid to the fish mixture. Fry the salt pork in a small heavy saucepan until golden brown. Add the onion. Cook slowly until the onion is translucent. Add the onion mixture to the fish mixture. Add the evaporated milk. Season with pepper. The chowder should be salty enough from the salt pork and quahogs, but more salt can be added if desired. Reheat slowly. Ladle into soup bowls or refrigerate and reheat later. The flavor of this chowder is best if it sets for several hours.
Yield: 6 servings

Mary Lou Garrett

BOUILLABAISSE NEW BEDFORD

4 (8-ounce) bottles clam juice
½ teaspoon thyme
½ teaspoon rosemary
½ teaspoon chervil
½ teaspoon fennel
1 medium bunch celery, chopped
1 (8-ounce) can tomato sauce
1 medium tomato, cut into 8 pieces
8 ounces cod, cut into 1-inch cubes
8 ounces haddock, cut into 1-inch cubes
8 ounces scallops, cut into halves, or 8 ounces whole bay scallops
8 littleneck clams, scrubbed

Pour the clam juice into a heavy 6- or 8-quart saucepan or kettle. Add the thyme, rosemary, chervil, fennel, celery, tomato sauce and tomato. Bring to a boil. Simmer for 15 minutes or until the celery is tender. Add the cod and scallops. Place the clams on top. Increase the heat. Boil for 10 minutes or until the clams open. Let stand over very low heat or place on a hot tray. Place 2 clams in each bowl. Ladle the fish and broth over the clams. Serve with rolls or French bread, a Bordeaux-type red wine and a light tossed salad with olive oil dressing.
Note: Herbs may be substituted freely and may be used in amounts to taste.
Any boned fresh fish may be substituted.
Yield: 4 servings

LOBSTER BISQUE

2 tablespoons butter
¼ cup diced carrot
1 rib celery, diced
1 onion, sliced
1 tablespoon parsley flakes
1½ cups lobster meat
⅓ cup dry white wine
½ cup chicken broth
3 tablespoons butter
¼ cup flour
3 cups boiling milk
3 tablespoons whipping cream
Salt and pepper to taste

Melt 2 tablespoons butter in a saucepan. Add the carrot, celery, onion, parsley and lobster. Cook for 5 minutes, stirring occasionally. Add the wine and chicken broth. Simmer for 20 minutes. Remove the lobster and cut into fine pieces; set aside. Set aside the vegetables in the cooking liquid. Melt 3 tablespoons butter in a large saucepan. Add the flour, blending with a wire whisk. Add the milk all at once, stirring vigorously with the wire whisk. Add the reserved vegetables and cooking liquid. Simmer, covered, for 1 hour. Strain through a fine sieve. Return to a boil. Add the cream, reserved lobster meat, salt and pepper.
Cook until heated through.
Yield: 6 to 8 servings
Jeanne Fabian

CHICK-PEA SOUP WITH CHOURICO AND SPINACH

2½ cups dried chick-peas
6 cups water
2 whole cloves
2 large yellow onions
2 cups water
2 medium potatoes, cubed
8 ounces chourico, thinly sliced
½ teaspoon coriander
½ teaspoon salt
½ teaspoon pepper
2 large bay leaves
4 large cloves of garlic, minced
½ teaspoon thyme
1 quart chicken stock
1 cup finely chopped spinach leaves

Rinse and sort the chick-peas. Combine with 6 cups water in a large kettle and soak overnight. Stick the cloves into the onions and set aside. Add 2 cups water to the undrained peas. Simmer over low heat for 4 to 5 hours or until the chick-peas are tender. Add the potatoes, chourico, coriander, salt, pepper, bay leaves, onions, garlic, thyme and chicken stock. Simmer for 25 minutes. Add the spinach. Simmer for 5 minutes. Remove from the heat. Remove the bay leaves and onions. Let stand until cool. Pour the soup into a blender container. Process until puréed. Return to the kettle. Reheat until warmed through.

Yield: 6 to 8 servings

Pamela J. Mackay

PORTUGUESE KALE SOUP

5 cups water
1 large shank bone
4 cloves of garlic, minced
1 onion, diced
1 rib celery, sliced
1 large bay leaf
2 packages frozen kale, or 4 cups fresh
1 cup sliced carrots
1 pound linguiça, sliced
1 pound chourico, sliced
3 to 5 cups water
3 large potatoes, diced
½ cup orzo
1 large can kidney beans, or 2 small cans
Salt and pepper to taste

Combine 5 cups water, shank bone, garlic, onion, celery and bay leaf in a large stockpot. Simmer for 20 to 30 minutes. Add the kale, carrots, linguiça, chourico and enough water to make of the desired consistency. Simmer for 20 minutes. Add the potatoes, orzo, undrained beans, salt and pepper. Simmer for 20 to 30 minutes. If possible, refrigerate the soup for 2 to 4 hours or overnight. Reheat to serve. Remove the bay leaf before serving. Serve with Portuguese bread.
Yield: 10 to 12 servings

Pamela J. Mackay

GREEN BEAN AND LINGUIÇA SOUP

¼ cup bacon drippings or
shortening
2 onions, chopped
1½ pounds linguiça, casing
removed, sliced

2 pounds fresh or frozen cut
green beans
1½ quarts (about) boiling water

Melt the bacon drippings in a large heavy saucepan. Add the onions. Cook until golden brown. Add the linguiça and green beans. Cook over medium heat for 45 minutes, stirring occasionally. Add just enough boiling water to cover the green beans and linguiça. Cook over low heat until the beans are tender. Note: There are no spices listed since the linguiça will provide the necessary flavoring. May add a chopped tomato if desired.
Yield: 6 to 8 servings
Elizette Quadros

EASY TURKEY SOUP

1 pound ground turkey
2 (14-ounce) cans chicken broth
1 quart water
1 envelope onion soup mix
2 ribs celery, chopped

1 (16-ounce) can chopped
tomatoes
1 (10-ounce) package frozen peas
and carrots
1 cup rice

Brown the turkey in a large nonstick saucepan, stirring until crumbly. Add the chicken broth, water, soup mix and celery. Boil for 20 minutes. Add the tomatoes, peas and carrots and rice. Cook until the rice is tender.
Yield: 4 to 6 servings
Gail Lee

HEARTS AND FAVA SALAD

1 (8-ounce) can artichoke hearts, drained
1 (14-ounce) can hearts of palm, drained
1 (20-ounce) can fava beans, drained, rinsed
5 scallions, chopped
2 cloves of garlic, mashed
½ cup olive oil
2 tablespoons lemon juice
1 teaspoon salt
½ teaspoon pepper

Cut the artichoke hearts into quarters. Cut the hearts of palm into ½-inch rounds. Combine the artichoke hearts, hearts of palm, fava beans and scallions in a large bowl and mix well. Combine the garlic, olive oil, lemon juice, salt and pepper in a small bowl, stirring until mixed. Pour the garlic mixture over the salad and toss. Marinate, covered, in the refrigerator for 2 hours or longer, stirring occasionally. Stir again just before serving time. May be prepared up to 1 day ahead.

Yield: 4 to 6 servings

Jack Stauder

BROCCOLI WHITE KIDNEY BEAN SALAD

2 tablespoons red wine vinegar
2 teaspoons olive oil
1 clove of garlic, minced
Salt and pepper to taste
¼ cup chopped roasted red
bell pepper

¼ cup chopped red onion
1½ cups chopped broccoli florets,
steamed, cooled
1 can white kidney beans

Combine the vinegar, olive oil, garlic, salt and pepper in a medium bowl and whisk together. Add the red pepper, onion, broccoli and beans and toss gently. Serve over a bed of lettuce if desired.
Yield: 2 to 3 servings
Tina Gaudette

FLORIDA COLESLAW

1 cup vinegar
2 cups sugar
½ cup salad oil
1 tablespoon celery seeds

1 teaspoon dry mustard
1 head cabbage, very finely
shredded

Combine the vinegar, sugar, oil, celery seeds and mustard in a saucepan. Boil until the sugar is dissolved, stirring frequently until well mixed. Pour over the cabbage in a large bowl and mix well. Chill overnight. Drain well before serving.
Yield: 4 to 6 servings
Lila M. Lister

Seaslaw Salad

3½ cups finely shredded
white cabbage
½ cup finely chopped green
bell pepper
1 small red onion, cut into
quarters, thinly sliced

¼ cup chopped fresh parsley
¼ cup chopped celery
2 cups chopped lobster or
cooked shrimp
¾ cup Lemon Sherry Vinaigrette

Combine the cabbage, green pepper, onion, parsley, celery, lobster and vinaigrette in a large bowl and toss gently with forks to mix. Chill, covered, for 2 hours or longer, stirring occasionally.
Yield: 6 servings
Marian R. Parsons

LEMON SHERRY VINAIGRETTE

3 tablespoons sherry
2 tablespoons fresh lemon juice
1 tablespoon red wine vinegar
1 tablespoon extra-virgin olive oil

2 teaspoons honey
4 fresh basil leaves, coarsely
chopped, or ¼ teaspoon dried

Combine the sherry, lemon juice, vinegar, olive oil, honey and basil in a blender container. Process until well mixed.

CUCUMBER SALAD

3 cucumbers (see Note)
Salt to taste
1 small onion, thinly sliced
½ cup cider vinegar
2 tablespoons vegetable oil
1 tablespoon sugar
2 tablespoons water
2 teaspoons caraway seeds
½ teaspoon paprika
Pepper to taste

Slice the cucumbers thinly on the slicing side of a grater. Sprinkle with salt. Let stand at room temperature for 1 hour; drain. Combine the cucumbers, onion, vinegar, oil, sugar, water, caraway seeds and paprika in a large bowl and mix well. Season with pepper and salt. Chill until serving time. Note: Cucumbers may be used peeled or unpeeled.
Yield: 4 to 6 servings

Andrea Dumas

FRESH SPINACH SALAD

1 pound fresh spinach, washed, chilled
¼ cup (or more) chopped green bell pepper
¼ cup (or more) chopped green onions
8 slices bacon
3 tablespoons brown sugar
2 tablespoons red wine vinegar
1 tablespoon lemon juice
1 tablespoon Worcestershire sauce
Minced garlic to taste
Salt to taste
2 hard-cooked eggs, finely chopped

Shred the spinach. Combine with the green pepper and green onions in a large bowl and mix well. Fry the bacon in a skillet until crisp. Remove the bacon to paper towels to drain. Add the brown sugar, vinegar, lemon juice, Worcestershire sauce, garlic and salt to the bacon drippings in the skillet and mix well. Pour over the salad greens. Crumble the bacon over the salad. Sprinkle with the eggs. Serve immediately.

Yield: 6 to 8 servings

Phyllis Carey

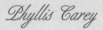

VEGETABLE HERB SALAD

4 cups shredded iceberg lettuce
2/3 cup chopped parsley
1 green or red bell pepper, seeded, chopped
2 cups coarsely chopped cauliflower or broccoli
2 large carrots, chopped
2 zucchini, chopped
1 cup mayonnaise
1 cup plain yogurt
2 tablespoons Dijon mustard
1 teaspoon dried rosemary
1 teaspoon dried basil
1 teaspoon dried oregano
2 teaspoons garlic salt
1/2 teaspoon pepper
2 1/2 cups shredded Cheddar cheese
2 green onions, thinly sliced
1/3 cup sunflower kernels

Layer the lettuce, parsley, green pepper, cauliflower, carrots and zucchini evenly in a large serving bowl. Combine the mayonnaise, yogurt, Dijon mustard, rosemary, basil, oregano, garlic salt and pepper in a bowl and mix well. Spread the mayonnaise mixture evenly over the salad. Sprinkle with the cheese, green onions and sunflower kernels. Chill, covered, for up to 24 hours.
Yield: 12 servings
Emily Thomson

SOUR CREAM AND CRANBERRY SALAD

1 can jellied cranberry sauce
1 cup hot water
2 (3-ounce) packages raspberry gelatin
1 cup boiling water
1 cup chopped pecans or walnuts
1 cup sour cream

Combine the cranberry sauce and hot water in a blender container. Process until liquefied and smooth. Dissolve the gelatin in the boiling water in a large bowl. Add the cranberry mixture and pecans to the gelatin. Pour half the gelatin mixture into an 8x8-inch pan or a mold. Freeze for 30 to 35 minutes or until firm. Spread the sour cream over the chilled gelatin. Top with the remaining gelatin mixture. Chill until firm. Cut into squares and serve on lettuce. May also serve on toast, English muffins or bagels.

Yield: 8 servings

Julie Blanchard

Combine cantaloupe and honeydew balls with strawberries and blueberries for a refreshing and colorful summer salad. Serve it in hollowed-out cantaloupe shells.

PASTA SALAD WITH HERB DRESSING

8 ounces spaghetti
4 medium tomatoes, peeled, cut
into quarters
1 medium cucumber, cut into
quarters, seeded

1 small green bell pepper, thinly
sliced
1 medium onion, thinly sliced
1 cup crumbled feta cheese
Herb Dressing

Cook the spaghetti using the package directions. Drain and let cool. Combine the tomatoes, cucumber, green pepper, onion and cheese in a large bowl and mix well. Add the spaghetti and mix well. Pour the dressing over the salad and toss lightly.
Yield: 6 to 8 servings
Colleen Gordon

HERB DRESSING

¼ cup salad oil
1 tablespoon sugar
3 tablespoons dry white wine
1 tablespoon snipped fresh basil,
or 1 teaspoon crushed dried basil

1 teaspoon salt
¼ teaspoon pepper
⅛ teaspoon Tabasco sauce
2 tablespoons lemon juice

Combine the oil, sugar, wine, basil, salt, pepper, Tabasco sauce and lemon juice in a glass jar. Cover and shake vigorously. May instead process in a blender until well mixed.

WALDORF SALAD

Juice of 1 lemon
10 tablespoons mayonnaise
Salt and pepper to taste
3 green apples, cored, diced

3 red apples, cored, diced
1 bunch celery, sliced
1 cup chopped walnuts
Lettuce leaves

Mix the lemon juice, mayonnaise, salt and pepper in a bowl. Add the apples and mix well.
Add the celery and walnuts just before serving time and mix well. Spoon onto a bed of lettuce.
Yield: 8 servings

Alice Henzel

TACO CRUNCH

1 pound ground beef
2 tomatoes, chopped
2 green bell peppers, chopped
1 head lettuce, torn into
bite-size pieces

½ cup shredded Cheddar cheese
1 can kidney beans, drained
1½ to 2 cups crushed
tortilla chips
Russian salad dressing to taste

Brown the ground beef in a skillet, stirring until crumbly; drain. Chill until needed. Combine
the tomatoes, green peppers, lettuce, cheese and beans in a large bowl and mix well. Chill for
1 hour or longer. Add the ground beef to the salad. Toss with the salad dressing.
Yield: 4 to 8 servings

Phyllis Sweeney

Meat, Poultry & Meatless Entrées

Wing's Neck Lighthouse

Originally built in *1849* at the end of Wing's Neck Peninsula, this station included a keeper's dwelling and oil house. A second keeper's house was moved from Ned Point light station in *1870*. In *1878*, a fire destroyed the tower and one of the keeper's dwellings, which was rebuilt in *1889*.

This lighthouse station received national attention in *1932* when the keepers, two brothers, saved eight lives between January *1* and August *30*.

Barbecued Beans

1 pound bacon, chopped
1 pound ground beef
1 onion, chopped
¼ cup prepared mustard
1 tablespoon chili powder
½ cup catsup
½ cup barbecue sauce

¼ cup molasses
1 teaspoon salt
¾ teaspoon pepper
2 (16-ounce) cans red beans
2 (16-ounce) cans pork and beans
2 (16-ounce) cans butter beans

Brown the bacon in a skillet; drain well. Brown the ground beef with the onion in the skillet, stirring until the ground beef is crumbly; drain well. Combine the bacon, ground beef mixture, mustard, chili powder, catsup, barbecue sauce, molasses, salt and pepper in the skillet. Simmer until heated through. Add all the beans and mix well. Pour into a 9x13-inch baking pan. Bake at 350 degrees for 1 hour.

Yield: 10 to 12 servings

Yvonne Mello

Pie à la Cheeseburger

1 pound ground beef
1½ cups chopped onions
1½ cups milk
¾ cup baking mix
3 eggs

½ teaspoon salt
¼ teaspoon pepper
1 small can stewed tomatoes or
peeled tomatoes
1 cup shredded Cheddar cheese

Brown the ground beef with the onions in a skillet, stirring until the ground beef is crumbly; drain. Spread in a greased 10-inch pie plate. Beat the milk, baking mix and eggs in a bowl until smooth. Add the salt and pepper. Pour over the ground beef mixture. Bake at 400 degrees for 25 minutes. Top with the tomatoes. Sprinkle with the cheese. Bake for 5 to 8 minutes longer or until the cheese melts.

Yield: 6 servings

Patricia H. Gardner

Beef Pocket Stroganoff

1½ pounds lean ground beef
1 tablespoon vegetable oil
⅓ cup diced onion
1 teaspoon melted butter
¼ cup thinly sliced fresh mushrooms
1 envelope instant beef broth and seasoning
1 teaspoon seasoned salt
1 teaspoon Worcestershire sauce
½ teaspoon salt
¼ teaspoon white pepper
2 cups sour cream, at room temperature
8 (1-ounce) sandwich pocket breads, heated slightly
Paprika to taste

Brown the ground beef in the oil in a skillet, stirring until crumbly; drain and set aside. Sauté the onion in the butter in a large skillet; do not brown. Add the mushrooms. Simmer for 5 minutes, stirring constantly. Stir in the beef broth and seasoning, seasoned salt, Worcestershire sauce, salt and pepper. Let cool until just warm. Add the sour cream and mix well. Warm over very low heat; the sour cream will curdle if the mixture is allowed to simmer. Slice open the pocket breads. Fill each pocket ⅔ full with the ground beef. Top with the sour cream mixture. Sprinkle with paprika.
Yield: 8 servings

Pat Cook

BURRITOS

½ cup (scant) shortening
3 cups flour
2 to 3 teaspoons salt
1 cup very warm water
1½ pounds ground beef
4 large potatoes, finely diced
½ cup finely chopped onion
2 tablespoons finely chopped celery, or ¼ teaspoon celery seeds
½ teaspoon salt
¼ teaspoon Greek oregano
⅛ teaspoon basil, or to taste
1½ to 2 cups shredded cheese of your choice

For the tortillas, cut the shortening into the flour and 2 to 3 teaspoons salt in a bowl until of uniform consistency. Add the water and mix until a soft dough forms. Let stand, covered, for 30 minutes. Divide the dough into 12 to 15 equal portions. Shape into balls. Knead each ball several times on a floured board. Roll 1 at a time to form tortillas. Cook the tortillas in a lightly oiled skillet over medium heat for 1½ minutes per side. The tortillas should be just barely brown and very flexible. Let the tortillas cool. Place in a sealable plastic bag and set aside. For the filling, combine the ground beef, potatoes, onion, celery, salt to taste, oregano and basil in a large saucepan. Add enough water to barely cover the ingredients. Bring to a boil; reduce the heat. Simmer for 25 minutes or until the potatoes are tender and the ground beef is cooked through. To assemble, reheat the tortillas a few at a time in a skillet until warm. Using a slotted spoon, place 3 tablespoons filling across the center of each tortilla. Sprinkle generously with cheese. Fold each tortilla in half; fold again lengthwise in half. Serve immediately.

Yield: 6 servings

Jean Beeler

LASAGNA WITH GOLDEN FLAKY TOPPING

2 pounds ground beef
½ cup chopped onion
2 (6-ounce) cans tomato paste
2 (8-ounce) cans tomato sauce
1 cup canned mushroom pieces and stems, drained
2 teaspoons crushed dried sweet basil
2 teaspoons dried parsley flakes
1 teaspoon salt
1 teaspoon oregano
½ teaspoon garlic salt
½ teaspoon pepper
2 cups creamed cottage cheese
2 cups chopped fresh spinach
2 cups shredded mozzarella cheese
2 cans flaky refrigerator biscuits or powder biscuits
2 tablespoons dried parsley flakes

Brown the ground beef with the onion in a skillet, stirring frequently; drain. Add the tomato paste, tomato sauce, mushrooms, basil, 2 teaspoons parsley flakes, salt, oregano, garlic salt and pepper and mix well. Simmer for 15 minutes. Mix the cottage cheese and spinach in a bowl. Alternate layers of the meat mixture, cottage cheese mixture and mozzarella cheese in two 8x12-inch baking dishes, ending with the cheese. Separate each biscuit into 3 layers. Arrange over the casseroles, overlapping the edges of the biscuits. Sprinkle each casserole with half the 2 tablespoons parsley flakes. Bake at 375 degrees for 25 to 30 minutes or until the topping is light golden brown. Serve hot.

Yield: 12 servings

Anne DaCruz

Marilyn's Marvelous Microwave Meat Loaf

1 small onion, chopped (optional)
1½ pounds lean ground beef or ground turkey
1 tablespoon catsup
1 teaspoon brown mustard
1 egg
¾ cup (about) seasoned bread crumbs
⅛ teaspoon Tabasco sauce, or to taste
1 teaspoon milk (optional)

Sauté the onion in a nonstick skillet until translucent. Combine the onion, ground beef, catsup, mustard, egg, bread crumbs, Tabasco sauce and milk in a large bowl and mix well. Shape into a loaf. Place in a glass baking dish. Cover tightly with plastic wrap. Microwave on High for 7 minutes. Uncover and add a small amount of catsup or other gravy to the top of the loaf. Microwave, uncovered, on High for 7 minutes. Remove from the microwave. Let stand for 1 minute. If the center of the loaf is not quite done, slice the loaf and cover tightly with plastic wrap. Microwave on High for 1 minute longer. Serve with mashed potatoes and vegetables or hot rice and a salad.

Yield: 4 servings

Marilyn Barros

Mom's Beef Rice Skillet

1 pound ground beef
1 onion, thinly sliced
1 green bell pepper, thinly sliced
1½ teaspoons salt
⅛ teaspoon pepper

1½ cups quick-cooking rice
1 (28-ounce) can tomatoes
½ teaspoon sugar, or
to taste
Shredded Cheddar cheese

Combine the ground beef, onion, green pepper, salt and pepper in a large skillet. Cook over medium heat until the ground beef is brown and crumbly, stirring frequently. Add the rice and tomatoes. Stir in the sugar if needed. Simmer for 5 minutes. Serve with the cheese.

Yield: 6 servings

Janice Sequeira

Ziti Bake

1 (16-ounce) package ziti
1 to 2 teaspoons olive oil
1½ to 2 pounds ground beef
1 green bell pepper, chopped
1 large onion, chopped
Italian seasoning to taste

Garlic powder to taste
Salt and pepper to taste
8 to 10 slices yellow American
cheese or other yellow cheese
1 large jar prepared spaghetti sauce
or pasta sauce

Combine the pasta, olive oil and water to cover in a large saucepan. Cook for 12 minutes; drain. Combine the ground beef, green pepper, onion, Italian seasoning, garlic powder, salt and pepper in a large skillet. Cook until the ground beef is brown, stirring frequently. Alternate layers of the ground beef mixture and pasta in a baking dish. Top with the cheese. Pour the spaghetti sauce over the top. Bake at 400 degrees for 30 to 40 minutes or until heated through.

Yield: 6 to 8 servings

Sharyn Fitzgerald

MEAL-IN-ONE FRIED RICE

1 large onion, cut into small pieces
3 ribs celery, cut into small pieces
1 cup bite-size pieces cooked roast beef or roast pork
2 teaspoons beef bouillon
½ cup soy sauce
1 cup uncooked converted long grain rice
2 tablespoons vegetable oil
1 cup boiling water

Sauté the onion and celery in a nonstick skillet until tender. Add the roast beef, bouillon and half the soy sauce. Add the remaining soy sauce, rice, oil and boiling water and mix well. Cook, tightly covered, over low heat for 15 minutes. If the rice is not tender, cook over low heat for 10 minutes longer or until the rice is tender and all the liquid is absorbed. Let stand, covered, for 5 to 10 minutes.
Yield: 4 to 6 servings

Geraldine M. Cardoza

Reheat cooked pasta or rice in a metal strainer over a pan of steaming water; cover with foil and steam for 15 minutes.

PEPPERED FILET MIGNON

1 (2-pound) filet mignon   Cracked black peppercorns
Virgin olive oil

Rub the entire filet generously with olive oil. Roll in peppercorns until coated.
Place on a broiler rack. Broil 6 inches from the heat source for 10 minutes per side.
Turn off the broiler. Let the filet stand in the oven for 5 minutes. Cut into thin slices.
Serve with the pan drippings.
Yield: 4 to 6 servings

Fran Liro

THIN FRIED STEAK À LA ROMANO

¼ cup olive oil   12 black olives, pitted, thinly sliced
½ medium onion, thinly sliced   ¼ teaspoon oregano
2 cloves of garlic, peeled,   Salt and pepper to taste
very thinly sliced   1 (1-pound) thin steak
⅔ cup chopped Italian tomatoes   Olive oil

Combine ¼ cup olive oil, onion, garlic, tomatoes, olives, oregano, salt and pepper in a saucepan.
Simmer for 15 minutes or until the tomatoes and olive oil separate. Fry the steak in a small amount
of olive oil in a skillet, turning it quickly and basting with the pan drippings. Remove the steak
to a hot platter. Pour the tomato sauce over the steak. Serve immediately.
Yield: 2 to 3 servings

Louise Jacoponi

STEAK SAN MARCO

2 pounds chuck steak, 1 inch thick, cut into serving pieces
1 envelope onion soup mix
1 (16-ounce) can peeled Italian tomatoes
1 large green pepper, cut into strips, or 2 small green peppers (optional)
1 teaspoon oregano
½ teaspoon garlic powder
¼ teaspoon salt
¼ teaspoon pepper
2 tablespoons vegetable oil
2 tablespoons wine vinegar
¼ cup wine (optional)

Place the steak in a large skillet. Cover with the soup mix. Add the tomatoes and green pepper strips. Sprinkle with the oregano, garlic powder, salt, pepper, oil and vinegar. Pour the wine over all the ingredients. Simmer, covered, for 1½ hours or until the steak is tender. Serve with rice. Note: Any canned green vegetables may be substituted for the green peppers but should not be added until the last 30 minutes of cooking time.
Yield: 4 to 6 servings

Mrs. Paula Benedetti

Steak Siciliano

1 cup burgundy
1 small clove of garlic, minced
1 small onion, minced
1 teaspoon Worcestershire sauce
2 tablespoons minced parsley
2 tablespoons butter
2 tablespoons prepared horseradish
2 tablespoons prepared mustard
1 tablespoon sugar
¼ teaspoon oregano
1 teaspoon salt
½ teaspoon pepper
1 (2½-pound) round steak, 1½ inches thick

Combine the burgundy, garlic, onion, Worcestershire sauce, parsley, butter, horseradish, mustard, sugar, oregano, salt and pepper in a small saucepan. Heat until the butter melts. Cool to room temperature. Pierce both sides of the steak deeply with a fork. Place in a shallow pan. Pour the burgundy mixture over the steak. Marinate in the refrigerator for several hours to overnight, turning occasionally. Remove the steak from the marinade. Remove the solids from the marinade with a slotted spoon and set aside. Broil the steak on 1 side, basting with the liquid from the marinade. Turn the steak. Spread with some of the marinade solids and baste with the liquid. Broil to desired degree of doneness. Note: Gravy may be prepared by adding a small amount of flour and water to the remaining marinade liquids in a saucepan. Cook until thickened, stirring constantly.
Yield: 6 to 8 servings

Nancy H. Wheeler

BRAZILIAN GRILLED LAMB AND BLACK BEANS

2 (15- or 16-ounce) cans black beans, rinsed, drained
½ cup cooked orzo
1 medium or large onion, finely chopped
1 tablespoon salsa
¼ teaspoon thyme
⅔ cup red wine vinaigrette salad dressing
½ well-trimmed butterflied leg of lamb (sirloin half)
2 teaspoons liquid smoke
1 teaspoon garlic salt
½ teaspoon ground red pepper
3 medium red or green bell peppers, seeded, cut into quarters
2 large oranges, peeled, cut into halves, sliced
12 corn tortillas

Line 1 or 2 baking pans with foil. Place a small grilling rack in each. Combine the beans, orzo, onion, salsa, thyme and half the salad dressing in a medium bowl. Mix well and set aside. Brush the lamb with the liquid smoke. Let stand for 5 to 10 minutes. Brush with the remaining salad dressing. Sprinkle evenly with the garlic salt and red pepper. Place the lamb and bell peppers on the racks in the prepared pans. Bake, covered with foil, at 450 degrees for 15 to 35 minutes or until the bell peppers are tender and the lamb registers 160 degrees on a meat thermometer, turning every 15 to 20 minutes. Remove the bell peppers from the pans if they are done before the lamb. Place the bean mixture in the center of a large serving platter. Arrange the bell peppers and oranges around the beans. Carve the lamb into thin slices. Arrange around the edge of the platter. Serve with the tortillas. Note: In the summertime, omit the liquid smoke and grill the lamb over hot coals.
Yield: 12 servings

Pamela J. Mackay

German Chops

8 center-cut pork chops,
3/4 inch thick
3 tablespoons vegetable oil
1 teaspoon salt
1/2 teaspoon pepper
4 cups sauerkraut

1 teaspoon caraway seeds
3 tablespoons honey
1/4 cup chopped onion
1 cup chopped apple
1/2 cup Rhine wine

Brown the pork chops in the oil in a large skillet. Season with salt and pepper. Mix the sauerkraut, caraway seeds, honey, onion, apple and wine in a bowl. Place in a saucepan. Arrange the pork chops over the sauerkraut mixture. Cook, covered, over low heat for 1 hour or until the pork chops are cooked through, basting with the pan drippings occasionally. Serve with chilled Rhine wine.

Yield: 4 servings

Barbecued Ribs

3 to 4 pounds spareribs
3/4 cup catsup
1/4 cup molasses
2 tablespoons minced onion
1/4 cup mustard

1/2 cup brown sugar
1/2 teaspoon pepper
3 cloves of garlic, chopped
1 teaspoon salt

Place the spareribs in a 9x13-inch baking pan. Mix the catsup, molasses, onion, mustard, brown sugar, pepper, garlic and salt in a bowl. Pour over the ribs, making sure the ribs are well covered. Marinate, covered with foil, in the refrigerator overnight. Bake, covered, at 375 degrees for 1 to 1 1/2 hours. Remove the foil. Bake for 30 minutes longer or until the ribs are cooked through.

Yield: 6 servings

Patricia H. Lopes

PORTUGUESE-STYLE PORK BUTTS AND RICE

2 cups port wine
1 teaspoon crushed red pepper
½ cup vinegar
Salt and black pepper to taste
5 pounds pork butts or fresh shoulders, cut into 3-inch pieces
1 green bell pepper, chopped
1 medium onion, chopped
2 cups water
2 cups quick-cooking rice
1 cup catsup

Mix the wine, red pepper, vinegar, salt and black pepper in a large container. Add the pork. Marinate in the refrigerator overnight. Place the pork and the marinade in a deep pan. Cook over medium heat until the pork is brown and the liquid has evaporated. Place the pork in a casserole; set aside. Sauté the remaining bits of the pork, green pepper and onion in the pan until the vegetables are tender. Add the water. Bring to a boil. Add the rice and catsup. Remove from the heat. Let stand for 7 minutes. Place the rice mixture in a second casserole. Bake both casseroles at 350 degrees for 10 to 15 minutes or until heated through.

Yield: 6 to 8 servings

Bernice Ann Alves

PORTUGUESE CACOILA

3 pounds pork blade meat, cut into 1½-inch pieces
12 ounces pork liver, cut into 1½-inch pieces
¼ cup cider vinegar
1 tablespoon salt
2 tablespoons chopped hot peppers
2 tablespoons pickling spice
2 tablespoons whole allspice
5 bay leaves, crushed
2 tablespoons garlic chips

Place the meat and liver in a 2-quart saucepan. Add enough water to reach ½ inch below the top of the meat. Add the vinegar, salt and peppers and mix well with a wooden spoon. Tie the pickling spice, allspice, bay leaves and garlic in a cheesecloth bag. "Bury" the bag in the center of the meat. Marinate in the refrigerator for 24 hours or longer. Remove the spice bag. Cook over low heat for 3 hours or until tender. Serve in Portuguese buns. Note: If desired, cubed potatoes may be added during the last 30 minutes of cooking time.

Yield: 8 to 10 servings

Mrs. John DeSouza

Saucisses au Chou (Sausage in Cabbage)

12 pork or beef sausages
1 large onion, sliced
1 cup green bell pepper, sliced lengthwise
2 apples, cut into sections
2 cups canned tomatoes
1½ cups cider
Salt and pepper to taste
1 head cabbage, finely chopped

Place a large skillet over high heat. Pour in a small amount of water. Add the sausages. Cook until the sausages are browned on all sides, turning occasionally. (The water in the skillet will evaporate and prevent the sausages from splitting.) Add the onion. Cook until translucent. Add the green pepper, apples, tomatoes, cider, salt and pepper. Cook for 10 minutes. Add the cabbage. Cook for 5 minutes. Note: This dish is economical, colorful and very easy to prepare.
Yield: 4 to 6 servings

Mrs. Drapeau

APRICOT-GLAZED HAM

1 (5- to 7-pound) fully cooked boneless ham
⅓ cup packed brown sugar
1 tablespoon cornstarch
½ teaspoon ground nutmeg
¼ teaspoon ground cloves
⅔ cup apricot nectar
2 teaspoons lemon juice

Place the ham on a rack in a shallow roasting pan. Insert a meat thermometer in the thickest part of the ham. Bake at 325 degrees for 1½ to 2 hours or until the meat thermometer registers 130 degrees. Combine the brown sugar, cornstarch, nutmeg and cloves in a small saucepan. Stir in the apricot nectar and lemon juice. Cook over medium heat until thickened and bubbly, stirring constantly. Brush the ham with the glaze. Bake for 15 to 20 minutes longer or until the meat thermometer registers 140 degrees, brushing occasionally with the glaze. Garnish with cooked baby artichokes and cooked baby carrots.
Yield: 15 to 20 servings

Peggy Bergman

Baked Beans and Ham Casserole

1 medium onion, peeled, chopped
1/4 cup chopped green bell pepper
1 cup cooked ham, julienned
2 tablespoons butter or margarine
1/2 cup tomato paste
1/2 cup water
1 tablespoon wine vinegar
1/2 teaspoon salt
1 (16-ounce) can baked beans
4 slices bacon

Sauté the onion, green pepper and ham in the butter in a skillet. Add the tomato paste, water, vinegar and salt. Simmer for 5 minutes. Add the beans. Pour into a 1-quart casserole. Arrange the bacon over the top. Bake at 350 degrees for 30 minutes or until bubbly and brown.

Yield: 4 to 6 servings

Sharyn Fitzgerald

CHICKEN AND BROCCOLI

3 chicken breasts
2 chicken bouillon cubes
1 (10-ounce) package frozen broccoli
1 pound Velveeta cheese
1 (10-ounce) can cream of chicken soup
1 (10-ounce) can cream of celery soup
1 (10-ounce) can cream of mushroom soup
1 small can evaporated milk
1 cup (about) bread crumbs
1 to 2 tablespoons butter
Paprika to taste

Rinse the chicken. Combine with the bouillon cubes and water to cover in a saucepan. Boil until cooked through. Let cool. Skin, debone and chop or slice the chicken. Cook the broccoli in water to cover in a saucepan for 5 to 6 minutes or just until tender-crisp; drain. Combine the cheese, soups and evaporated milk in a double boiler. Cook until the cheese melts, stirring frequently. Layer the broccoli and chicken in a 2-quart casserole. Pour the cheese sauce over the top. Top with the bread crumbs. Dot with the butter. Sprinkle with paprika. Bake at 350 degrees for 20 to 25 minutes or until heated through.

Yield: 4 to 6 servings

M. Lucille Negus

CHICKEN BREAST SCAMPI

2 to 3 pounds boneless chicken breasts
2 tablespoons margarine
2 tablespoons olive oil
1 small onion, diced
1 teaspoon minced garlic
¼ teaspoon salt
⅛ teaspoon pepper
½ teaspoon dried parsley

Rinse the chicken and pat dry. Place in a baking dish and set aside. Heat the margarine and olive oil in a skillet over low heat until the margarine melts. Add the onion, garlic, salt, pepper and parsley. Sauté until the onion is translucent. Pour the onion mixture over the chicken. Bake, covered, at 350 degrees for 1 hour. Bake, uncovered, for 20 minutes or until the top is light golden brown and the chicken is cooked through. Serve with linguini smothered with Alfredo sauce.
Yield: 6 to 8 servings

Jan Barrette

GREEK-STYLE CHICKEN WITH LEMON SAUCE

2 cups seasoned bread crumbs
1 tablespoon parsley flakes
¼ cup chopped walnuts
Salt to taste
⅛ teaspoon pepper
1 egg
2 tablespoons butter

⅓ cup finely chopped celery
⅓ cup finely chopped onion
6 boneless chicken breasts
2 tablespoons butter
¼ cup fresh lemon juice
Lemon Sauce

Mix the bread crumbs, parsley flakes, walnuts, salt, pepper and egg in a medium bowl and set aside. Melt 2 tablespoons butter in a saucepan over low heat. Add the celery and onion. Sauté for 2 minutes. Add the sautéed mixture to the bread crumb mixture and mix well. Rinse the chicken and pat dry. Lay the chicken on a flat dry surface. Place a layer of stuffing on each piece. Roll up and secure with wooden picks. Place in a lightly greased 8x12-inch baking pan. Heat 2 tablespoons butter and lemon juice in a small saucepan until the butter melts. Bake the chicken at 350 degrees for 1 hour or until cooked through, brushing occasionally with the butter mixture. Remove the wooden picks. Pour the lemon sauce over the chicken at serving time.

Yield: 6 servings

Barbara Johansen

LEMON SAUCE

3 egg yolks
2 tablespoons melted butter
¼ cup fresh lemon juice

1½ to 2 cups chicken broth
Flour

Beat the egg yolks in a bowl. Add the butter, lemon juice and 1½ cups of the chicken broth. Pour into a saucepan. Stir in a small amount of flour. Cook until thickened, adding the remaining ½ cup chicken broth if needed.

Mexican Chicken

4 pounds chicken breasts
3 cups water
1 tablespoon salt
1 tablespoon butter
1 medium Bermuda onion, chopped
2 green bell peppers, finely chopped
1 clove of garlic, minced
1 (16-ounce) can tomatoes
2 small cans button mushrooms, drained
¼ cup parsley
1 teaspoon chili powder
½ teaspoon oregano

Rinse the chicken. Combine with the water and salt in a saucepan. Cover and bring to a boil. Simmer, covered, for 45 to 60 minutes or until tender and cooked through. Let the chicken cool in the broth. Debone the chicken and tear into large pieces. Boil the broth, uncovered, until reduced to 2 cups. Strain the broth and set aside. Melt the butter in a skillet. Add the onion, green peppers and garlic. Sauté until the vegetables are tender. Add the tomatoes, mushrooms, parsley, chili powder, oregano and chicken broth. Add the chicken. Cook until heated through.
Yield: 10 to 12 servings

STIR-FRIED CHICKEN AND VEGETABLES

1 medium chicken breast
1 tablespoon vegetable oil
4 medium mushrooms, sliced
1 small carrot, sliced
10 fresh snow peas
2 green onions, sliced
¼ cup bean sprouts
½ tablespoon cornstarch
¼ cup chicken broth or bouillon
1 teaspoon soy sauce
½ teaspoon garlic powder

Rinse the chicken and pat dry. Debone and cut into bite-size pieces. Heat the oil in a skillet. Add the chicken. Stir-fry the chicken until no pink remains. Add the mushrooms and carrot. Stir-fry for 2 minutes. Add the snow peas, green onions and bean sprouts. Stir-fry for 2 minutes. Mix the cornstarch with a small amount of cold water. Add the cornstarch, chicken broth, soy sauce and garlic powder to the skillet. Cook until a sauce forms, stirring constantly. Boil for 1 minute, stirring constantly. Serve over steamed white rice.

Yield: 1 serving

Richard Benoit

CHICKEN ENCHILADA CASSEROLE

1½ boneless chicken breasts
8 slices American cheese,
    cut into halves
1 (10-ounce) can cream of
    chicken soup

2 cups sour cream
7 (8-inch) flour tortillas, torn into
    5 to 6 pieces each
⅓ cup coarsely chopped fresh or
    canned jalapeños

Rinse the chicken. Simmer in water to cover in a shallow saucepan for 30 minutes or until cooked through. Reserve ¾ cup of the chicken stock. Cut the chicken into bite-size pieces. Reserve some of the cheese for the topping. Alternate layers of the soup, reserved chicken stock, chicken, the remaining cheese, sour cream, tortillas and jalapeños in an 8x11-inch casserole until all the ingredients are used. Top with the remaining cheese. Bake at 375 degrees for 35 to 45 minutes or until heated through. Serve with salad and rolls.

Yield: 4 servings

Libby Russell

SAVORY BAKED CHICKEN

1 (3-pound) chicken, cut up, or
    equivalent amount of boneless
    chicken breasts
1 (8-ounce) bottle creamy Russian
    salad dressing

1 envelope onion soup mix
1 (8- to 10-ounce) jar
    apricot preserves

Rinse the chicken and pat dry. Place in a roasting pan. Mix the salad dressing, soup mix and preserves in a bowl. Pour over the chicken. Bake, covered, at 300 degrees for 1 hour or until the chicken is cooked through. Note: May marinate the chicken in the salad dressing mixture in the refrigerator for 1 hour. Let stand for several minutes before baking.

Yield: 4 to 6 servings

Eva McCarthy
Deborah A. Szala Cicchetti

SAVORY MARINATED CHICKEN

1 broiler-fryer, cut up
1 cup wine vinegar
1 cup water
2 cloves of garlic, crushed
1 tablespoon crushed red pepper
1 onion, sliced
2 tablespoons olive oil
¼ cup catsup
1 cup rice
Salt and black pepper to taste

Rinse the chicken and pat dry. Combine the vinegar, water, garlic and red pepper in a large bowl. Add the chicken. Marinate in the refrigerator for 6 hours to overnight, turning at least once. Drain and discard the marinade. Sauté the onion in the olive oil in a large skillet. Add the chicken and enough water to cover. Stir in the catsup. Cook until the chicken is tender and almost cooked through. Add the rice. Cook until the chicken is cooked through and the rice has absorbed all the sauce. Season with salt and pepper.

Yield: 4 to 6 servings

Olga Jason

CHICKEN POTPIE

1 chicken
1 can mixed vegetables, drained
1 medium onion, chopped
2 (10-ounce) cans cream of chicken soup
1 (10-ounce) can cream of mushroom soup
1 cup flour
1 cup milk
¾ cup mayonnaise

Rinse the chicken and pat dry. Debone, skin and chop the chicken. Arrange the chicken in a 9x13-inch baking pan. Add the mixed vegetables and onion. Combine the chicken soup and mushroom soup in a bowl and mix until smooth. Pour over the chicken. Combine the flour, milk and mayonnaise in a bowl and mix well. Pour over the chicken. Bake at 350 degrees for 1 hour or until brown. Note: The flour mixture will seem thin and watery, but it will bake into a crust.

Yield: 4 to 6 servings

Yvonne Mello

CHICKEN AND RICE

1 chicken, cut up
1 cup rice
1 (10-ounce) can cream of mushroom soup
1 (10-ounce) can cream of celery soup
1 envelope onion soup mix
2 cups water

Rinse the chicken and pat dry. Place the chicken and rice in a 9x13-inch baking pan.
Pour the mushroom soup and celery soup over the chicken and rice. Sprinkle with the soup mix.
Pour the water over the top. Seal the pan with a double thickness of foil. Bake at 325 degrees
for 2 1/4 hours or until the chicken is cooked through.
Yield: 8 to 10 servings

Joan Hall

For a quick treat, coat chicken pieces with baking mix and a
mixture of spices. Arrange in melted butter in a baking pan and
bake until the chicken is cooked through.

Glazed Turkey

1 to 2 cloves of garlic, minced, or to taste
1 to 2 tablespoons (or more) butter or margarine
Salt, pepper and paprika to taste
1 to 2 bay leaves
Vegetable oil
1 (14- to 16-pound) turkey
1 pound sliced bacon
1½ cups white wine
1 cup brandy

Combine the garlic, butter, salt, pepper, paprika and bay leaves in a saucepan. Add enough oil to make of the desired consistency. Simmer until heated through. Rinse the turkey and pat dry. Pierce several times with a large fork. Place the turkey in a roasting pan. Brush the simmered mixture over the turkey. Cover with the bacon. Pour the wine and brandy over the turkey. Roast at 325 degrees for 4½ to 5½ hours or until the turkey is cooked through, basting with the pan juices occasionally.

Yield: 14 to 16 servings

Yvonne Mello

LOW-CAL SPINACH CHEESE MANICOTTI

1 cup diced onion
½ cup canned chicken broth
1 (28-ounce) can Italian plum tomatoes
¼ cup tomato sauce
2 teaspoons sugar
2 cloves of garlic, minced, or ¼ teaspoon instant minced garlic
¼ teaspoon salt
¼ teaspoon oregano
¼ teaspoon basil
⅛ teaspoon pepper
10 manicotti tubes
1 (10-ounce) package frozen chopped spinach
1 cup low-fat cottage cheese
1 cup part-skim-milk ricotta cheese
2 tablespoons grated Parmesan cheese
2 eggs, beaten
¼ teaspoon salt
⅛ teaspoon pepper
⅛ teaspoon nutmeg, or to taste

For the sauce, cook the onion in the chicken broth in a heavy saucepan over medium heat until the onion is translucent. Add the tomatoes, tomato sauce, sugar, garlic, ¼ teaspoon salt, oregano, basil and ⅛ teaspoon pepper and mix well. Bring to a boil; reduce the heat. Simmer, covered, for 10 minutes. Simmer, uncovered, for 10 minutes longer. Cook the manicotti using the package directions; drain. For the filling, cook the spinach using the package directions; drain. Combine with the cottage cheese, ricotta cheese, Parmesan cheese, eggs, ¼ teaspoon salt, ⅛ teaspoon pepper and nutmeg in a bowl and mix well. Stuff the filling into the manicotti with a spoon or pastry bag. Spread ½ cup of the sauce in a 9x13-inch baking pan. Add the manicotti. Cover with the remaining sauce. Bake at 350 degrees for 20 minutes or until heated through.

Yield: 5 servings

Colleen Gordon

69

SPINACH LASAGNA

1 pound ricotta cheese
2 cups shredded mozzarella cheese
1 egg
1 package frozen chopped spinach, thawed
½ teaspoon salt
½ teaspoon oregano
½ teaspoon pepper
1 (32-ounce) jar spaghetti sauce
8 lasagna noodles
1 cup water

Combine the ricotta cheese, half the mozzarella cheese, egg, spinach, salt, oregano and pepper in a large bowl and mix well. Layer 1 cup spaghetti sauce, 4 lasagna noodles and half the spinach mixture in a greased 9x13-inch baking pan. Repeat the layers. Top with the remaining spaghetti sauce. Sprinkle with the remaining 1 cup mozzarella cheese. Pour the water around the edges of the pan. Bake, covered tightly with foil, at 350 degrees for 1¼ hours. Let stand for 15 minutes before serving.

Yield: 8 to 10 servings

Jerilyn Czapiga

PASTA PRIMAVERA

1 (12-ounce) package rotini primavera
3 small zucchini, thinly sliced
1 medium green or red bell pepper, cut into ½-inch chunks
¼ teaspoon minced garlic
¼ cup vegetable oil
1 teaspoon salt
⅛ teaspoon crushed red pepper
12 to 15 pea pods, trimmed
1 (2-ounce) can sliced olives, drained
¼ cup grated Parmesan cheese
3 tablespoons minced parsley
10 to 12 cherry tomatoes, cut into halves

Cook the pasta using the package directions. Drain and keep warm. Sauté the zucchini, green pepper and garlic in the oil in a skillet over medium heat for 5 minutes. Add the zucchini mixture to the pasta. Add the salt and pepper and toss to blend. Stir in the pea pods and olives. Chill until serving time. Add the cheese, parsley and tomatoes just before serving. Toss well.
Yield: 4 to 6 servings
Carol Rodrigues

Vegetarian Casserole

2 cups wide egg noodles
2 tablespoons vegetable oil
1 rib celery, chopped
1 medium onion, chopped
1 small green bell pepper, chopped
1½ cups shredded Monterey Jack cheese
1 cup cooked broccoli cuts
½ cup milk
¾ teaspoon salt
⅛ teaspoon pepper
¼ cup fine dry bread crumbs
2 tablespoons shredded Cheddar cheese
1 tablespoon wheat germ
1 tablespoon melted butter or margarine

Cook the noodles using the package directions; drain. Heat the oil in a skillet. Add the celery, onion and green pepper. Cook until tender but not brown. Stir in the noodles, Monterey Jack cheese, broccoli, milk, salt and pepper. Pour into a 1½-quart casserole. Bake, covered, at 350 degrees for 15 minutes. Combine the bread crumbs, Cheddar cheese, wheat germ and butter in a bowl and mix well. Sprinkle around the edges of the casserole. Bake, uncovered, for 10 minutes.
Yield: 4 servings

Janice M. Tapper

BROCCOLI SURPRISE

1 (10-ounce) package chopped
broccoli
⅓ cup milk
1 (10-ounce) can cream of
mushroom soup

1 cup herb-flavored stuffing mix
½ cup shredded sharp
Cheddar cheese

Combine the broccoli, milk, soup, stuffing mix and cheese in a bowl and mix well.
Pour into a casserole. Bake at 325 degrees for 45 minutes.
Yield: 4 to 6 servings

Joan Hall

SUMMER SQUASH CASSEROLE

6 cups sliced summer squash or
zucchini
¼ cup chopped onion
1 (10-ounce) can cream of
chicken soup

1 cup sour cream
1 cup grated carrot
1 package stove-top stuffing mix
½ cup melted butter or margarine

Combine the squash, onion and water to cover in a saucepan. Boil for 5 minutes; drain.
Add the soup, sour cream and carrot. Combine the stuffing mix and butter in a bowl and mix
well. Spread half the stuffing in a 10x13-inch casserole. Add the squash mixture. Top with
the remaining stuffing. Bake at 350 degrees for 30 minutes.
Yield: 6 servings

Mrs. Kathleen Galas

VEGETARIAN PIE

1 unbaked pie shell
2 packages frozen chopped broccoli
1 onion, chopped
1 (4-ounce) can mushrooms, drained
2 tablespoons butter or margarine
1 egg, beaten
4 slices American cheese
1 (9-ounce) can yams in heavy syrup
1 tablespoon butter or margarine
1 unbaked pie pastry

Bake the pie shell at 425 degrees for 10 minutes. Cook the broccoli using the package directions; drain. Sauté the onion and mushrooms in 2 tablespoons butter in a skillet. Combine the onion mixture and broccoli in a bowl and mix well. Stir in the egg. Pour into the pie shell. Cover with the cheese. Mash the yams with 1 tablespoon butter in a bowl. Spread over the cheese. Cut the pie pastry into strips. Interweave over the top of the pie.
Bake at 425 degrees until the top is brown.
Yield: 6 to 8 servings

Mrs. Maureen Billington

Babchi Szala's Pierogies with Cabbage Filling

6 eggs	5 pounds flour
1 quart milk	Cabbage Filling
2 to 3 teaspoons (or more) salt	Butter

Beat the eggs in a large bowl. Add the milk and salt. Add half the flour and mix well. Add the remaining flour gradually, mixing well after each addition. Knead on a floured surface until the dough is elastic and no longer sticky. Let rest, covered with a cloth, until needed. Roll very thin on a floured surface. Cut the dough with a 3- to 4-inch cookie cutter. Roll and reshape the remaining dough until all is used. Place a large spoonful of cabbage filling in the center of each circle. Fold the dough carefully in half over the filling, being careful not to make any holes in the dough. Pinch the edges to seal. Drop the pierogies several at a time into boiling water in a large saucepan. Boil until the pierogies float to the top. Melt butter in a large skillet. Add several pierogies at a time. Fry until golden brown.

Yield: 20 to 30 servings

Joann, Mike, Tom and Amy Szala

CABBAGE FILLING

1 head cabbage	½ cup butter
1 can sauerkraut	Salt and pepper to taste
2 large onions, ground	

Combine the cabbage and undrained sauerkraut in a saucepan. Boil for 20 minutes. Drain and let cool. Grind the cabbage and sauerkraut together. Sauté the onions in the butter in a skillet until tender. Combine the cabbage mixture, onions, salt and pepper in a bowl and mix well.

Tostado Pizza

2 tablespoons yellow cornmeal
2 cups baking mix
½ cup cold water
1 pound ground beef
¾ cup water
3 tablespoons chopped seeded canned green chiles
1 envelope taco seasoning mix
1 (15-ounce) can refried beans
1 cup shredded sharp American cheese
1 cup shredded lettuce
1 tomato, chopped
½ cup chopped onion
Taco sauce (optional)

Sprinkle the cornmeal over a greased 12-inch pizza pan. Combine the baking mix and ½ cup water in a bowl. Mix with a fork until the dough forms a ball. Knead on a lightly floured surface 5 or 6 times. Roll into a 14-inch circle. Pat onto the prepared pan. Crimp the edges. Brown the ground beef in a skillet, stirring until crumbly; drain. Add ¾ cup water, green chiles and taco seasoning mix. Bring to a boil; reduce the heat. Simmer for 15 minutes or until thick. Spread the beans over the dough. Top with the ground beef mixture. Bake at 450 degrees for 18 to 20 minutes or until light brown. Top with the cheese. Bake for 4 minutes longer or until the cheese melts. Cut into 6 wedges. Garnish with fresh green chiles. Serve the lettuce, tomato and onion separately. Drizzle with taco sauce.
Yield: 6 servings

Mrs. Maureen Billington

VEGETARIAN TORTILLAS

3 medium zucchini, chopped
3 medium yellow squash, chopped
1 cup chopped onion
3 to 4 cloves of garlic, pressed
8 ounces cream cheese
1½ cups shredded Cheddar cheese
12 tortillas
4 cups sour cream
1 large jar salsa

Combine the zucchini, squash, onion and garlic in a medium saucepan. Add the cream cheese and Cheddar cheese. Cook until the cheese melts, stirring frequently. Cook the tortillas using the package directions. Have the guests fill the tortillas with the vegetable mixture. Top with spoonfuls of sour cream and salsa. Note: This is a very messy dish.
Serve with large napkins.
Yield: 6 servings

Jacqueline Crosby

RICE AND PIGEON PEAS

3 tablespoons vegetable oil
2 tablespoons salt
⅓ can tomato sauce
¼ cup sofrito
1 package Sazon (achiote seeds)
¼ teaspoon garlic powder
1 can pigeon peas
4 cups water
4 cups rice

Combine the oil, salt, tomato sauce, sofrito, Sazon and garlic powder in a saucepan. Cook over low heat until very hot. Add the peas with liquid and mix well. Increase the heat to high. Add the water. Bring to a boil. Add the rice; reduce the heat to medium. Cook for 7 minutes or until the rice has absorbed all the liquid. Mix well. Reduce the heat to low. Cook, covered, for 12 minutes. Watch carefully to prevent burning.

Yield: 4 servings

Maria Hernandez

ORZO WITH FETA CHEESE

2 teaspoons olive oil
2 cups chopped onion
2 cloves of garlic, minced
1½ cups orzo
2 cans vegetable broth
½ cup crumbled feta cheese
¼ cup grated Parmesan cheese
½ cup chopped fresh parsley
Salt and pepper to taste

Heat the olive oil in a saucepan. Add the onion and garlic. Sauté over low heat. Stir in the rice. Add the broth. Cook, covered, until the rice is tender and the liquid is absorbed, stirring frequently. Remove from the heat. Stir in the cheeses and parsley. Season with salt and pepper. Spoon into a serving bowl. Serve warm.

Yield: 4 to 6 servings

Tina Gaudette

TABOULI

1 cup bulgur (cracked wheat)
2 cups cold water
2 bunches fresh parsley, removed from stems, chopped
1 bunch scallions, cut into small pieces
4 large tomatoes, cut into very small pieces
1 tablespoon allspice
½ teaspoon cinnamon
½ cup vegetable oil
Juice of 2 lemons
Salt to taste

Soak the bulgur in the water in a bowl for 30 minutes. Drain well, squeezing out excess water.
Stir in the parsley, scallions, tomatoes, allspice, cinnamon, oil, lemon juice and salt.
Mix well. Chill, covered, for 2 hours.
Yield: 12 servings
Florence Morad

Seafood Entrées

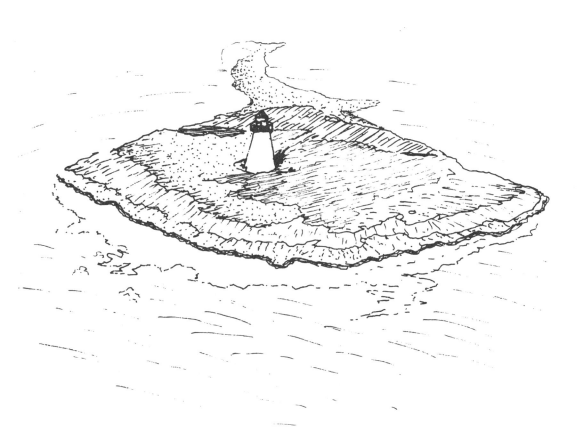

Bird Island Lighthouse

This lighthouse built in 1819 on Bird Island is just south of Butler Point on the east side of Sippican Harbor and is now a private navigational aid.

A hurricane in 1938 destroyed the dwelling attached and other buildings on the island. The high-water mark from the hurricane reached sixteen feet up from the foundation of the twenty-five-foot light tower.

BAKED FISH CREOLE

⅔ cup water
⅓ cup butter
2 cups herb-flavor stuffing mix
1 (1-pound) fish fillet (1 inch thick), cut into 4 pieces
1 (8-ounce) can stewed tomatoes, cut into small pieces
1 (8-ounce) can tomato sauce
1 teaspoon sugar
1 small onion, chopped
½ teaspoon garlic powder
½ teaspoon oregano
¼ teaspoon salt

Bring the water and butter to a boil in a saucepan over medium heat. Add the stuffing mix and mix well. Place 4 equal scoops of the stuffing in a buttered casserole. Arrange the fish over the stuffing. Bake, covered with foil, at 350 degrees for 30 minutes. Combine the tomatoes, tomato sauce, sugar, onion, garlic powder, oregano and salt in a medium saucepan. Bring to a boil over medium heat. Simmer, covered, over low heat while the fish is baking. Pour the sauce over the fish. Serve hot.

Yield: 4 servings

Debra Pickup

CODFISH DELIGHT

2 pounds salted boneless cod
¾ cup vegetable oil
3 large onions, sliced into rings
1 tablespoon ground red pepper
1 large green bell pepper, chopped
1 tablespoon parsley
½ cup tomato sauce
¼ cup white wine

Soak the codfish in water to cover in the refrigerator for 2 days, changing the water occasionally. Combine the codfish with clean water to cover in a saucepan. Bring to a boil. Remove the codfish to a baking dish. Break the fish into chunks. Heat the oil in a saucepan. Add the onions, red pepper, green pepper and parsley. Cook until the onions are tender. Pour the sauce over the fish. Let cool. Add the tomato sauce and wine and mix well. Bake at 400 degrees for 40 minutes or until golden brown, turning once.

Yield: 4 servings

Clotilde Rapoza

Fresh Codfish Balls

½ cup water
1 pound baking potatoes, cut into 1-inch pieces
1 pound fresh or frozen cod fillets, cut into 2-inch pieces
Vegetable oil for frying
½ cup fresh bread crumbs
1 egg
2 tablespoons butter, softened
½ teaspoon salt
⅛ teaspoon pepper

Bring the water to a boil in a medium saucepan. Add the potatoes. Cook, covered, over low heat for 15 minutes or until tender. Add the fish. Cook, covered, over low heat for 3 minutes or until the fish flakes easily. Heat 3 inches of oil to 375 degrees in a medium saucepan. Drain the fish mixture. Add the bread crumbs, egg, butter, salt and pepper. Beat with a potato masher or hand-held mixer until smooth. Shape by 2 tablespoonfuls into balls. Drop several at a time into the hot oil. Fry for 3 to 5 minutes or until golden brown. Drain well on all-natural paper towels. Serve with cocktail sauce.

Yield: 4 servings

Diane J. Senna

SIMPLE CODFISH CAKES

2 small potatoes or 1 large potato, cooked, mashed
1 can codfish mix, flaked
2 tablespoons finely chopped parsley
1 tablespoon ground red pepper
1 small onion, finely chopped
2 eggs
Vegetable oil for frying
Cocktail sauce

Combine the potatoes and codfish in a bowl and mix well. Add the parsley, pepper and onion and mix well. Stir in the eggs. Shape into patties or balls. Heat the oil in a skillet. Add the fish patties several at a time. Fry until golden brown. Drain on paper towels. Dip in cocktail sauce.
Yield: 3 to 4 servings

Dorothy E. Oliviera

Flake leftover fish into a white sauce, add canned peas and carrots, and serve in patty shells.

CRAB-STUFFED FLOUNDER WITH CHEESE SAUCE

2 cups prepared herb-flavor stuffing mix
8 ounces crab meat
2 pounds flounder fillets (see Note)
3 tablespoons melted butter or margarine
1 tablespoon lemon juice
1 package cheese sauce mix

Combine the stuffing and crab meat in a bowl and mix well. Place the fish in a 2-inch-deep baking dish. Drizzle with some of the butter. Place a heaping serving of stuffing on each piece of fish. Roll up and secure with wooden picks. Drizzle the remaining butter and lemon juice over each roll. Bake at 350 degrees for 30 minutes. Prepare the cheese sauce using the package directions. Spoon the sauce over each portion of fish at serving time.
Note: If using frozen fish, thaw before using.
Yield: 4 servings

Mrs. Terry Francouer

OVEN-FRIED FISH

1 pound haddock fillets
½ cup low-calorie French salad dressing
½ cup seasoned bread crumbs

Marinate the fish in the salad dressing in a dish for 15 minutes, turning frequently. Sprinkle the bread crumbs in a shallow pan. Press each fillet in the crumbs, coating each side lightly. Arrange the fish in a single layer on a baking sheet sprayed with nonstick cooking spray. Bake at 450 degrees for 8 to 10 minutes or until the fish flakes easily, turning carefully after 6 minutes.

Yield: 2 servings

Sandra Harrison

For a salt-free Cajun spice mix for seafood, grind together 1 cup paprika, ¼ cup cayenne, ¼ cup freshly ground black pepper, 2 tablespoons oregano, 2 thyme leaves, 2 tablespoons onion powder, 1 tablespoon celery seeds, and 1½ teaspoons garlic powder. This also makes a great gift for friends.

STUFFED FISH FILLETS

2 pounds fresh haddock or cod fillets
½ teaspoon salt
Juice of 1 lemon or equivalent juice concentrate
1 (16-ounce) can peeled tomatoes, strained (see Note)
1 large onion, sliced into very thin rings
1 teaspoon crushed rosemary leaves
1 teaspoon oregano
4 slices Swiss cheese
Melted butter

Rinse the fish and pat dry. Sprinkle with the salt. Drizzle with the lemon juice. Cut the fish into 4 equal pieces. Arrange 2 pieces in a microwave-safe 10-inch skillet. Flatten the tomatoes and arrange over the fish. Top with the onion rings. Sprinkle with the rosemary and oregano. Add the cheese. Place the remaining fish over the cheese. Microwave, covered, for 15 minutes or until the fish flakes easily, turning ½ turn after 7 minutes; do not overcook. Turn off the microwave. Let the fish stand in the microwave for several minutes. Arrange the fish on a platter. Brush with melted butter. Garnish with parsley. Serve with rice and mixed vegetables. Note: Tomato paste may be substituted for the tomatoes.

Yield: 4 servings

Mrs. Irene Costa

SHANGHAI SALMON

2 (8-ounce) center-cut salmon fillets
Salt and pepper to taste
1 tablespoon vegetable oil
8 shiitake mushroom caps, thinly sliced
2 scallions, finely chopped
1 shallot, minced
2 tablespoons finely chopped peeled fresh ginger
1 lemon wedge
3 tablespoons chablis or sherry
½ cup whipping cream

Season the salmon lightly with salt and pepper. Heat a skillet over high heat until very hot. Add the oil. Add the salmon carefully. Cook for 1 minute or until seared. Turn and sear the other side. Remove the salmon to an ovenproof dish. Bake at 400 degrees until easily flaked. Combine the mushroom caps, scallions, shallot and ginger in a saucepan. Cook until the mushroom caps begin to wilt. Squeeze the lemon juice into the saucepan. Stir in the wine to deglaze the saucepan. Cook until reduced by ½, stirring occasionally. Add the cream. Cook for 1 minute or until the sauce thickens, stirring constantly. Place 1 salmon fillet in the center of each of 2 serving plates.
Cover with the cream sauce.
Yield: 2 servings

Christine McEnaney

SALMON LOAF WITH PARSLEY SAUCE

1 (16-ounce) can salmon
¾ cup soft bread crumbs
½ teaspoon salt
⅛ teaspoon pepper

1 tablespoon melted butter
1 egg
2 tablespoons milk
Parsley Sauce

Remove all skin and bone from the salmon. Reserve the liquid. Combine the salmon, reserved liquid, bread crumbs, salt, pepper and butter in a large bowl and mix well. Beat the egg slightly with the milk. Add to the salmon mixture. Pack into a buttered small loaf pan. Bake at 400 degrees for 40 minutes. Unmold onto a platter. Serve with the parsley sauce.
Yield: 4 servings

Dolores Gomes

PARSLEY SAUCE

2 tablespoons butter
2 tablespoons flour
1 cup milk

½ teaspoon salt
⅛ teaspoon pepper
2 tablespoons minced parsley

Blend the butter and flour in a double boiler over boiling water. Add the milk gradually, stirring constantly. Cook until the sauce thickens, stirring constantly. Cook for 5 minutes longer.
Add the salt, pepper and parsley.
Makes 1¼ cups sauce.

MARINATED SWORDFISH

1 cup vegetable oil
Juice of 2 lemons
2 tablespoons white wine vinegar
1 teaspoon salt
1/4 teaspoon pepper
1/2 teaspoon dried basil
1/8 teaspoon cayenne
1 clove of garlic, minced
1 pound fresh swordfish

Combine the oil, lemon juice, vinegar, salt, pepper, basil, cayenne and garlic in a
medium bowl and mix well. Pour half the mixture into an oblong glass 2-quart casserole.
Add the fish. Cover with the remaining mixture. Marinate, covered, in the refrigerator
for 4 hours or longer. Remove the fish from the marinade. Discard the marinade.
Place the fish in a broiler pan or on foil. Broil for 20 minutes. May instead be grilled if desired.
Adjust cooking time accordingly.

Yield: 2 servings

Pam Barao

HERBED TROUT BAKE

1 pound fresh or partially frozen
trout
¼ cup chopped onion
1 small clove of garlic, minced
2 tablespoons butter or margarine

½ teaspoon tarragon
½ teaspoon parsley
¼ teaspoon thyme
½ teaspoon salt
¼ cup cracker crumbs

*Place the fish in a greased lasagna pan. Sauté the onion and garlic in the butter in a skillet.
Stir in the tarragon, parsley, thyme and salt. Simmer for 1 minute.
Spread the mixture over the fish. Top with the cracker crumbs. Bake at 475 degrees for
10 to 12 minutes or until the fish flakes easily.
Yield: 4 servings*

Beverly Tavares

MY OWN NEW ENGLAND STUFFED QUAHOGS

2 tablespoons butter or margarine
1 small onion, diced
1 can minced clams
8 slices white bread, cut into
small cubes
1 teaspoon poultry seasoning

1 teaspoon salt
1 teaspoon garlic salt
½ teaspoon pepper
Empty quahog shells
Melted butter

*Melt 2 tablespoons butter in a skillet over low heat. Add the onion. Sauté until tender.
Add the clams and clam juice. Add the bread cubes and a small amount of water to moisten
gradually. Stir until well mixed. Add the poultry seasoning, salt, garlic salt and pepper. Fill the
quahog shells with the mixture. Sprinkle with a small amount of melted butter.
Yield: 4 to 6 servings*

Dianne Doyle

CLAMS AND MUSSELS STEAMED WITH HOT PEPPER AND GARLIC

¼ cup olive oil
5 cloves of fresh garlic, crushed
1 teaspoon red pepper flakes or chopped red pepper
1 cup chopped clams, including the liquor
1 cup shucked mussels, including the liquor
3 tablespoons chopped fresh parsley
1 teaspoon oregano
5 tablespoons white sherry, dry red wine or water
⅛ teaspoon salt, or to taste

Heat the olive oil in a large skillet. Add the garlic. Sauté until tender. Add the pepper flakes. Sauté for 1 minute. Add the clams, mussels, parsley and oregano. Add the sherry. Cook, covered, for 6 to 7 minutes or until the seafood is cooked through. Season with the salt. Serve hot or cold with crusty French or Italian bread.

Yield: 4 servings

Joan Carlsen

MUSSELS PORTUGUESE-STYLE

3 pounds mussels
¼ cup olive oil
3 bay leaves
1 tablespoon chopped garlic
1 medium onion, diced
½ green bell pepper, diced
½ red bell pepper, diced
2 medium tomatoes, chopped
4 ounces ground linguiça
1 cup white wine
2 tablespoons chopped parsley
2 tablespoons chopped cilantro
Pepper to taste

Wash the mussels and remove the beards. Soak in water to cover for 15 minutes. Heat the olive oil in a large skillet. Add the bay leaves, garlic, onion, green pepper and red pepper. Cook for 5 minutes or until the vegetables are tender. Add the tomatoes, linguiça and wine. Simmer for 5 minutes. Drain the mussels and add to the skillet. Steam, covered, for 6 minutes or until cooked through. Remove the mussels to a bowl. Add the parsley, cilantro and pepper to the sauce. Spoon the sauce over the mussels.
Yield: 4 servings
Rhonda Arno

Pasta with Seafood Extravaganza

½ cup extra-virgin olive oil
1 red bell pepper, sliced
1 green or yellow bell pepper, sliced
4 ounces snow peas, tips removed
Florets of 1 small bunch broccoli
2 to 3 cloves of garlic, chopped
2 tablespoons butter
2 teaspoons chopped parsley
8 ounces bay scallops
8 ounces medium shrimp, peeled, deveined
8 ounces fettuccini, cooked (see Note)
4 ounces feta cheese, crumbled
4 ounces Parmesan cheese, grated

Heat 1 teaspoon of the olive oil in a skillet. Add the bell peppers and snow peas. Stir-fry until tender-crisp. Set aside. Steam the broccoli for 5 minutes. Set aside. Sauté the garlic in the remaining olive oil and butter in a skillet until tender. Add the parsley, scallops and shrimp. Cook over medium heat for 4 to 5 minutes or until the shrimp turn pink. Keep warm over low heat. Toss the vegetables, seafood and pasta in a large bowl. Add the feta cheese and toss. Serve immediately with the Parmesan cheese. Note: Fresh tomato-basil fettuccini is best in this recipe. Prepare the pasta according to the package directions, timing it to finish at the same time as the seafood.

Yield: 2 servings

Betty-Ann Costa

New Bedford Seafood en Croute with Lobsterdaise Sauce

12 slices bacon
6 littleneck clams
Chopped parsley to taste
10 ounces mushrooms, coarsely chopped
1 medium yellow onion, coarsely chopped
4 scallions, 4 inches long, coarsely chopped
2 medium cloves of garlic, coarsely chopped
½ cup butter
⅓ cup chablis
6 scallops (10 scallops or fewer per pound)
Buttery Pastry (page 97)
¾ teaspoon (about) flour
Lobsterdaise Sauce (page 97)

Fry the bacon until crisp; set aside. Shuck the clams, reserving the liquid. Combine the clams, parsley, mushrooms, onion, scallions and garlic in a blender container or food processor container. Process until puréed. Strain through a sieve. Mix the strained liquid with the reserved clam liquid. Melt butter in a large saucepan over low heat. Add the puréed mixture. Increase the heat to high. Bring to a boil. Add the wine and reduce the heat. Simmer for 5 minutes. Remove from the heat and let cool. Strain through a sieve. Mix the strained liquid with the reserved clam liquid; reserve to use in the Lobsterdaise Sauce. Wrap each scallop with 2 bacon slices. Secure with wooden picks. Roll the pastry into six 8x8-inch squares. Place a pinch of flour in the center of 1 square. Place 1 tablespoonful of the puréed mixture over the flour. (The flour will absorb any excess moisture, leaving the dough dry.) Place 1 scallop over the puréed mixture. Remove the wooden pick. Fold the corners of the dough to the center, covering the entire scallop. Seal the corners with a small amount of water. Repeat with the remaining scallops and dough. Place seam side down in a buttered casserole. Bake at 325 degrees for 20 minutes or until the pastry is golden brown. Serve with the Lobsterdaise Sauce.
Yield: 2 to 3 servings

Mr. Jones

LOBSTERDAISE SAUCE

3 egg yolks
⅛ lemon
⅛ teaspoon Tabasco sauce,
   or to taste
2 tablespoons reserved clam liquid

⅛ teaspoon freshly ground white
   pepper, or to taste
1 cup butter
4 ounces steamed lobster meat

Place the egg yolks in a large bowl. Squeeze in the lemon juice. Add the Tabasco sauce, clam juice and pepper and mix gently. Bring 2 inches of water to a boil in the bottom of a double boiler over high heat. Set the bowl over the double boiler. Cook until thickened, whipping constantly. Remove from the heat. Melt the butter in a small saucepan over medium-high heat. Add the lobster meat and reduce the heat. Simmer for 2 minutes. Remove from the heat. Remove 1 tablespoon melted butter at a time and add slowly to the egg mixture, whipping constantly; do not mix in any solids at this point. When only lobster meat and solids remain, remove the lobster meat with a fork. Fold into the sauce.
Serve with New Bedford Seafood en Croute.
Yield: 1½ to 2 cups

BUTTERY PASTRY

1 cup butter
2 cups flour

1 teaspoon salt
¼ cup cold water

Cut butter into very small pieces. Sift the flour and salt onto a board. Add butter and enough cold water to form a dough, mixing well.

PORTUGUESE-STYLE PAELLA

2 (2-pound) broiler-fryers, cut into 8 pieces each
½ cup vegetable oil
1 pound lean pork, cut into 1-inch cubes
2 cups chopped onions
2 cloves of garlic, crushed
¼ teaspoon pepper
1 teaspoon dried oregano
Salt to taste
2 cups long grain rice
½ teaspoon saffron
1 pound linguiça, cut into halves
2 medium tomatoes, chopped
1 bay leaf
3 cans chicken broth
1½ pounds large shrimp, peeled, deveined
1 package frozen peas

Rinse the chicken and pat dry. Heat the oil in a large skillet. Add 5 pieces of chicken
at a time. Cook until golden brown, removing each piece to paper towels as it browns. Place the
pork cubes in the skillet. Cook until browned on all sides. Remove and set aside. Place the onions,
garlic, pepper and oregano in the skillet. Sauté for 5 minutes or until the onions are golden brown.
Add the salt, rice and saffron. Cook for 10 minutes, stirring constantly. Cook the sausage in
another skillet for 10 minutes or until brown on all sides, turning frequently; drain. Place the
chicken, pork cubes and sausage in a roasting pan. Add the tomatoes, bay leaf and chicken broth
to the rice mixture. Bring to a boil. Add the shrimp. Add ½ cup water if the mixture seems too
dry. Spoon evenly over the chicken, sausage and pork. Bake, tightly covered with foil, at
375 degrees for 1 hour. Remove the foil. Sprinkle the peas over the top without stirring.
Bake for 20 minutes longer. Remove to a serving platter. Discard the bay leaf.
Garnish with ½ jar pimentos and wedges cut from 2 lemons.
Yield: 10 to 12 servings

Mary Ann Gomes

SHRIMP PANSIT

1 pound narrow egg noodles
2½ tablespoons sesame oil
1 cup finely chopped white onion
Minced garlic to taste
8 ounces ground pork fat or fatback
1½ cups finely shredded green cabbage
½ cup thinly sliced scallions
1 pound shrimp, peeled, deveined (about 16 to 20 shrimp)
1½ cups (or more) beef stock
¼ teaspoon grated ginger
¾ teaspoon salt
¼ teaspoon ground black pepper
⅛ teaspoon cayenne, or to taste
¼ teaspoon nutmeg
3 tablespoons soy sauce

Cook the noodles in water to cover in a saucepan; drain and set aside. Heat the oil in a large sauté pan. Add the onion and garlic. Sauté until tender but not brown. Add the pork fat, cabbage, scallions and shrimp and mix well. Add the beef stock. Simmer for 10 minutes or until the shrimp turn pink and the vegetables are crisp. Mix the ginger, salt, black pepper, cayenne and nutmeg in a bowl. Add the soy sauce and mix well. Add the soy sauce mixture to the shrimp mixture. Cook until the vegetables are tender, adding a small amount of beef stock if needed to keep the mixture moist. Remove all the solids and half the liquid from the sauté pan. Set aside and keep warm. Add the noodles to the remaining sauce and toss gently. Spoon the noodles onto a platter. Top with the shrimp mixture.
Garnish with additional thinly sliced scallions.
Yield: 4 servings

Jason B. Ward

Squid Portuguese

1 tablespoon olive oil
1 onion, peeled, minced
1 clove of garlic, peeled, minced
2 tablespoons dry sherry
2 tablespoons tomato sauce
4 ounces fresh small mushrooms, cleaned, sliced
¼ teaspoon dried rosemary
1 tablespoon chopped parsley
Salt and pepper to taste
1½ pounds squid, cleaned, skinned, cut into cubes

Heat the olive oil in a heavy skillet. Add the onion and garlic. Cook over low heat for 10 minutes, stirring occasionally. Mix the sherry with enough water to measure ½ cup. Combine with the tomato sauce, mushrooms, rosemary, parsley, salt and pepper in a bowl and mix well. Stir the mushroom mixture into the onion mixture. Add the squid. Cook, covered, over low heat for 30 minutes or until the squid is tender when pierced with a fork.
Yield: 4 servings

Mrs. George Jason Jr.

Breads

Tarpaulin Cove Lighthouse

Tarpaulin Cove lighthouse was established in 1817 on the southwesterly shore of Naushon Island. The tower now standing was built in 1856 and the other buildings were demolished in 1962 due to deterioration.

Tarpaulin Cove was widely used in sailing days as a shelter during storms or while vessels awaited favorable winds. During the 17th century, a small village was located there and pirates used it as a base to prey on shipping in the Sound.

APPLE CIDER CRANBERRY BREAD

2 cups sifted flour
²⁄₃ cup sugar
½ teaspoon baking soda
1½ teaspoons baking powder
¼ teaspoon salt
¾ cup apple cider, heated
1 egg, beaten
2 tablespoons vegetable oil
1½ cups coarsely chopped fresh cranberries
½ cup coarsely chopped pecans

Mix the flour, sugar, baking soda, baking powder and salt in a large bowl. Add the cider, stirring just until moistened. Add the egg and oil, stirring just until mixed. Fold in the cranberries and pecans. Pour into a buttered loaf pan. Bake at 325 degrees for 1 hour or until a wooden pick inserted near the center comes out clean. Cool completely. Wrap in plastic wrap or foil and store at room temperature for 1 day before serving.

Yield: 1 loaf

Cynthia Pacheco

Beer Linguiça Bread

3 cups self-rising flour
3 tablespoons sugar
1 egg
1 (12-ounce) can or bottle beer, at room temperature
8 ounces ground linguiça

Combine the flour, sugar, egg, beer and linguiça in a bowl and mix thoroughly; do not beat. Pour into a greased and floured loaf pan. Bake at 375 degrees for 55 to 60 minutes or until the loaf tests done.

Yield: 1 loaf

Florence Hathaway

To knead bread dough, fold the dough toward you, then push it away with the heels of your hands in a rocking motion. Rotate it a quarter turn and repeat until the dough is springy and blistered with tiny bubbles under the surface and smooth on top.

BROWN BREAD

1 cup all-purpose flour
2 teaspoons baking soda
½ teaspoon salt
2 cups graham flour
½ cup sugar
½ cup bran
½ cup molasses
2 cups sour milk

Sift the all-purpose flour, baking soda and salt into a large bowl and mix well. Add the graham flour, sugar and bran and mix well. Add the molasses and milk and beat until smooth. Pour into a greased loaf pan. Let stand for 20 minutes. Bake at 300 degrees for 1 to 1¼ hours.

Yield: 1 loaf

Rose Lawton

CHEESE HERB BREAD

2 cups all-purpose flour
½ teaspoon salt
2 teaspoons baking powder
½ teaspoon baking soda
½ teaspoon dried basil
¼ teaspoon dried oregano
⅛ teaspoon thyme, or to taste
¼ cup butter or margarine
2 eggs
¼ cup honey
¾ cup milk
1 cup shredded Cheddar cheese

Combine the flour, salt, baking powder and baking soda in a bowl. Add the basil, oregano and thyme and mix well. Cut in the butter with a pastry blender or 2 knives until crumbly. Beat the eggs, honey, milk and cheese in a small bowl until well mixed. Add the egg mixture to the flour mixture, stirring just until mixed. Pour into a greased 8-inch round baking pan. Bake at 350 degrees for 45 to 55 minutes or until the top springs back when lightly touched. Cool in the pan. Cut into wedges.
Yield: 8 to 10 servings

Mrs. Maureen Billington

CORNMEAL, ONION AND CHEESE BATTER BREAD

1 cup yellow cornmeal
1¼ teaspoons salt
2 teaspoons baking powder
2 cups milk
2 eggs
¼ cup finely chopped onion
1 cup boiling water
2 tablespoons vegetable oil
½ cup shredded sharp cheese
3 tablespoons sesame seeds

Combine the cornmeal, salt and baking powder in a greased 1½-quart casserole. Stir in the milk, eggs and onion and beat well with a wire whisk. Stir in the water, oil and cheese and mix well. Sprinkle with the sesame seeds. Bake at 375 degrees for 35 minutes or until puffed and golden brown. Serve immediately.
Yield: 6 to 8 servings

Mrs. Frederick J. Joerres

FRENCH BREAD

2 packages dry yeast
1 cup scalded milk, cooled
2 eggs
¼ cup honey
5 cups flour
2 teaspoons salt
1 egg, beaten

Dissolve the yeast in the milk in a large bowl. Add 2 eggs and honey and beat thoroughly.
Sift in 4 cups of the flour and salt and mix well, adding additional flour if needed. Knead on a
floured board until smooth and elastic. Place in a buttered bowl, turning to coat the surface.
Let rise, covered, until doubled. Punch the dough down, pressing out all the air.
Shape into 2 long loaves on a floured board. Place on a buttered baking sheet.
Brush with the beaten egg. Let rise for 30 minutes or until doubled.
Bake at 400 degrees for 20 to 25 minutes or until the loaves test done.
Yield: 2 loaves

Barbara E. Moss

ORANGE BREAD

2 cups flour
1 tablespoon baking powder
½ teaspoon salt
5 tablespoons butter, softened
½ cup sugar
1 egg, beaten
3 tablespoons grated orange peel
½ cup water
½ cup orange juice

Sift the flour, baking powder and salt together. Beat the butter in a mixer bowl.
Add the sugar gradually, beating constantly until light and fluffy.
Add the egg and orange peel. Add the water, orange juice and flour mixture
alternately, beating well after each addition. Pour into a greased 4x8-inch loaf pan.
Let stand for 20 minutes. Bake at 350 degrees for 55 to 60 minutes.
Yield: 1 loaf

Mrs. Harold Harrop

OLD NEW BEDFORD POTATO BREAD

1½ pounds baking potatoes
2 envelopes dry yeast
3 tablespoons warm water
2 tablespoons olive oil
3¾ to 4 cups flour
1½ teaspoons salt
1 tablespoon water

Combine the potatoes with water to cover in a saucepan. Boil until tender.
Peel and mash the potatoes while still warm. Stir the yeast into the warm water. Let stand for
10 minutes. Combine the potatoes, yeast, olive oil, flour and salt in a large mixer bowl.
Beat for 3 minutes. Add up to 1 tablespoon water gradually, mixing until the dough
forms a ball. Knead on a floured surface for 5 minutes. Place the dough in an oiled bowl,
turning to coat the surface. Cover with plastic wrap. Let rise in a draft-free place
for 1½ hours. Flour a baking sheet heavily. Sprinkle with cornmeal. Cut the dough into
2 equal portions. Shape each portion into a round loaf. Slit the tops of the loaves. Place the
loaves side by side on the prepared baking sheet. Let rise for 45 minutes or until doubled in bulk.
Place the baking sheet in a 450-degree oven. Reduce the oven temperature to 400 degrees.
Bake for 35 to 40 minutes or until the loaves test done. Mist the loaves with water
3 times during the first 10 minutes of baking.
Yield: 2 loaves

Nancy Moreira

PORTUGUESE SWEET BREAD

½ cup butter
1 cup sugar
1½ teaspoons salt
1 cup milk, heated
1 cake yeast
¼ cup lukewarm water
4 large eggs or 5 small eggs, beaten
½ teaspoon ground mace
5 to 6 cups flour

Combine the butter, sugar, salt and milk in a large bowl, stirring until the sugar and salt are dissolved. Cool to lukewarm. Dissolve the yeast in the lukewarm water. Add the yeast, eggs and mace to the sugar mixture. Add the flour gradually, mixing well after each addition until a smooth dough forms. Let stand in a warm place overnight. Punch the dough down. Knead on a lightly floured surface. Shape into loaves in 2 greased loaf pans. Let rise for 1 hour. Bake at 350 degrees for 1 hour. Cool in the pans for 5 minutes. Remove to a wire rack. Cover with a towel and cool completely.

Yield: 2 loaves

Donna Medeiros

SWEDISH RAISIN RYE LOAVES

1¾ cups boiling water
⅓ cup packed dark brown sugar
¼ cup quick-cooking or rolled oats
¼ cup butter, softened
¼ cup dark molasses
1 tablespoon salt
2 teaspoons caraway seeds
1 teaspoon anise seeds
1 envelope dry yeast
¼ cup warm (105 to 115 degrees) water
3 cups unbleached all-purpose flour
3 cups rye flour
1 cup golden raisins or mixed dark and golden raisins
1 egg white, beaten
2 teaspoons caraway seeds (optional)

Combine the boiling water, brown sugar, oats, butter, molasses, salt, 2 teaspoons caraway seeds and anise seeds in a large bowl and mix well. Cool to lukewarm. Stir the yeast into the warm water. Add to the brown sugar mixture. Add about 2½ cups of the all-purpose flour and beat until smooth. Blend in the rye flour and enough of the remaining all-purpose flour to form a smooth dough. Turn onto a lightly floured board. Cover with the bowl. Let stand for 10 minutes. Knead in the raisins. Knead until smooth and elastic. Place in a greased bowl, turning to coat the surface. Cover with plastic wrap and a hot damp towel. Let rise in a warm place until doubled in bulk. Punch the dough down. Let rise for 30 minutes. Punch the dough down. Divide the dough into 2 equal portions. Shape into 2 loaves. Place in 2 greased 5x9-inch loaf pans. Let rise, covered with plastic wrap, until doubled in bulk. Brush the tops of the bread lightly with the egg white. Sprinkle with 2 teaspoons caraway seeds. Bake at 375 degrees for 40 minutes or until the loaves are very brown and sound hollow when tapped. Remove to a wire rack immediately to cool.
Yield: 2 loaves

Patricia Anne Costa

Malasadas
(Portuguese Fried Dough)

1 envelope dry yeast
1 teaspoon sugar
⅓ cup warm water
5 to 6 cups flour
1 teaspoon salt
½ cup sugar
1⅓ cups light cream
6 tablespoons melted butter
4 eggs, at room temperature
Vegetable oil

Dissolve the yeast and 1 teaspoon sugar in the warm water. Combine the flour, salt and ½ cup sugar in a large bowl, mixing well with a wooden spoon. Add the cream and butter and mix well. Add the eggs and yeast. Mix until a soft dough forms. Cover and let rise in a warm place until doubled in size. Punch the dough down or stir down. The dough will be sticky. Let rise a second time. Stir the dough down. Heat the oil to 425 degrees in a skillet. Drop the dough by spoonfuls into the hot oil. Fry until light brown on both sides; drain. Dip in additional sugar.

Yield: 2 to 3 dozen

Phyllis R. Souza

HIGH-FIBER PERFECTION MUFFINS

2¼ cups oat bran cereal
3 tablespoons brown sugar
1 tablespoon baking powder
½ teaspoon cinnamon
¼ teaspoon mace
¼ teaspoon vanilla extract
2 egg whites
¼ cup safflower oil or canola oil
¾ cup evaporated skim milk
1 very ripe large pear or 2 small pears, peeled, cored

Combine the cereal, brown sugar, baking powder, cinnamon and mace in a large bowl and mix well. Combine the vanilla, egg whites, oil, evaporated milk and pear in a blender container. Process at low speed until mixed. Add the pear mixture to the brown sugar mixture and mix well. Pour into 12 paper-lined muffin cups. Bake at 425 degrees for 17 minutes or until a wooden pick inserted in a muffin comes out clean.

Yield: 1 dozen

Dot Manny

ONION ROLLS

1 envelope dry yeast
¼ cup warm water
1 cup milk
1 teaspoon salt
2 tablespoons sugar
¼ cup butter
3¼ to 3½ cups flour
2 medium onions, sliced paper thin
2 tablespoons butter
1 egg yolk, beaten
¼ cup sour cream
½ teaspoon salt

Dissolve the yeast in the warm water. Heat the milk in a saucepan. Add 1 teaspoon salt, sugar and ¼ cup butter. Let cool. Stir in the yeast. Add 2½ cups of the flour and beat until smooth. Add the remaining flour, beating until a soft dough forms. Cover and let rise. Cook the onions in 2 tablespoons butter in a skillet for 10 minutes. Knead the dough on a floured surface for 10 minutes. Shape into balls. Place the balls 3 inches apart on 2 greased baking sheets. Press the onions into the dough. Spread a mixture of the egg yolk, sour cream and ½ teaspoon salt over the onions. Let rise again. Bake at 350 degrees for 20 to 25 minutes or until brown.
Yield: 1 dozen

Mary Cabral

Fabulous Veggie Rolls

2 envelopes dry yeast
1½ cups warm (105 to 115 degrees) water
½ cup sugar
1 tablespoon salt
2 eggs
½ cup butter, softened
½ cup warm mashed potatoes
6½ cups flour
Melted butter
1 medium carrot, grated
1 cup chopped onion
¼ cup butter
1 cup chopped fresh mushrooms
Poppy seeds to taste
Sesame seeds to taste

Sprinkle the yeast over the warm water in a large bowl. Add the sugar and salt, stirring until dissolved. Let stand until the yeast bubbles. Add the eggs, ½ cup butter, potatoes and 3 cups of the flour, mixing with a wooden spoon until smooth. Add 2 cups of the flour, stirring until mixed. Add enough of the remaining flour to form a smooth dough. Brush the top of the dough with melted butter. Cover with waxed paper and a towel. Let rise in the refrigerator for 2 hours or until doubled in bulk. Combine the carrot, onion and ¼ cup butter in a skillet. Cook until the onion begins to soften. Add the mushrooms. Cook for 1 to 2 minutes. Two hours before serving time, punch the dough down and divide into 2 equal portions. Roll each portion ½ inch thick on a floured surface. Spread each with half the carrot mixture. Roll up as for jelly rolls. Cut into 1½-inch slices. Place cut side down on a greased baking sheet. Brush with additional melted butter. Sprinkle with the poppy seeds and sesame seeds. Let rise, covered with a towel, for 1 hour. Bake at 400 degrees for 12 minutes or until brown.
Yield: 5 to 6 dozen

Lorraine G. Carr

Easter Egg Ring

½ cup milk
2 tablespoons butter
¼ cup sugar
1 teaspoon salt
1 envelope dry yeast
¼ cup very warm water
1 egg, beaten
3 cups flour
3 drops of oil of anise
5 or 6 uncooked white-shell eggs
Easter egg coloring

Heat the milk and butter in a saucepan until the milk is scalded. Stir in the sugar and salt. Dissolve the yeast in the warm water in a large bowl. Stir in the milk mixture and the beaten egg. Beat in 1 cup of the flour until smooth. Beat in the oil of anise. Beat in enough of the remaining flour to form a stiff dough. Knead the dough on a floured surface until smooth and elastic, adding additional flour if needed. Place the dough in a greased bowl, turning to coat the surface. Let rise, covered with a towel, for 1 hour or until doubled in bulk. Tint the remaining eggs while the dough is rising. Punch the dough down. Place on a floured board and divide into 6 equal portions. Shape each portion into a 12-inch-long roll. Shape 3 rolls into a braid on a baking sheet. Repeat with the remaining 3 rolls. Form a circle with the braids; pinch the ends together. Place the eggs large end up in the braids, spacing evenly. Let rise, covered, for 1 hour or until doubled in bulk. Bake at 375 degrees for 30 minutes.

Yield: 6 to 12 servings

Donna Cunha

Desserts

Ned Point Lighthouse

This still-active light was built in 1837 using whitewashed stone and set on four acres of land in Mattapoisett. The original station included a keeper's dwelling and barn, an oil house, and the lighthouse tower.

The keeper's dwelling was moved by barge in 1930 to the Wing's Neck Light Station in Pocasset.

Cape Cod Blueberry Meringue Cake

1½ cups flour
1 teaspoon baking powder
¼ teaspoon salt
½ cup butter or margarine, softened
1 cup sugar
2 egg yolks
½ cup milk
1 teaspoon vanilla extract
1½ cups fresh blueberries
2 egg whites
¼ cup sugar
½ teaspoon vanilla extract

Sift the flour, baking powder and salt together. Cream the butter and 1 cup sugar in a mixer bowl until light and fluffy. Beat in the egg yolks. Add the flour mixture and milk alternately to the creamed mixture, beating well after each addition. Stir in 1 teaspoon vanilla. Pour half the batter in a greased 9x12-inch cake pan. Sprinkle with the blueberries. Cover with the remaining batter. Bake at 350 degrees for 35 minutes. Beat the egg whites in a mixer bowl until foamy. Add ¼ cup sugar and ½ teaspoon vanilla gradually, beating constantly until stiff peaks form. Increase the oven temperature to 400 degrees. Spread the meringue over the warm cake. Bake for 10 minutes or until the meringue is golden brown. Note: May substitute frozen blueberries for the fresh blueberries; do not thaw before using.

Yield: 12 servings

Eleanor Roth

FRESH SOUR CREAM CRANBERRY CAKE

2 cups flour
1 teaspoon baking powder
1 teaspoon baking soda
½ teaspoon salt
½ cup margarine, softened
1 cup sugar

3 eggs
1 cup sour cream
1 teaspoon vanilla extract
2 cups chopped cranberries
Brown sugar to taste
Cinnamon to taste

Sift the flour, baking powder, baking soda and salt together. Cream the margarine and sugar in a mixer bowl until light and fluffy. Beat in the eggs 1 at a time. Add the flour mixture and sour cream alternately to the creamed mixture, beating well after each addition. Stir in the vanilla and half the cranberries. Pour half the batter into a greased 10-inch tube pan. Cover with the remaining cranberries and batter. Sprinkle lightly with brown sugar and cinnamon. Bake at 325 degrees for 1 hour.

Yield: 16 servings

Mary Cabral

DEVILISH GRAND MARNIER CAKE

1 (2-layer) package devil's food
cake mix
3 tablespoons Grand
Marnier liqueur
1¼ cups sifted confectioners' sugar

8 ounces whipped cream
cheese, softened
½ teaspoon vanilla extract
1½ cups whipping cream

Prepare the cake mix using the package directions and adding 1 tablespoon of the liqueur to the liquid. Pour into 3 greased and floured 9-inch cake pans. Bake as directed. For the filling, blend ½ cup of the confectioners' sugar into the cream cheese in a large mixer bowl. Beat in the remaining 2 tablespoons liqueur and vanilla. Beat in the remaining confectioners' sugar. Add the whipping cream. Beat until stiff peaks form. Place 1 cake layer on a platter. Spread with ⅓ of the cream mixture. Repeat with the remaining layers and cream mixture. Garnish with chocolate curls. Chill until serving time.

Yield: 16 servings

Germaine Varieur

Glazed Holiday Gift Cakes

1 cup margarine, softened
8 ounces cream cheese, softened
1½ cups sugar
1½ teaspoons vanilla extract
4 eggs
2 cups flour
1½ teaspoons baking powder
¾ cup chopped pecans or walnuts
¾ cup chopped cherries
2 tablespoons milk
1½ cups confectioners' sugar

Cream the margarine and cream cheese in a mixer bowl until light and fluffy.
Add the sugar and vanilla and mix well. Add the eggs 1 at a time, beating well after each
addition. Add 1¾ cups of the flour and baking powder gradually, mixing well after
each addition. Mix the pecans, cherries and remaining ¼ cup flour in a small bowl. Fold into
the batter. Pour the batter into 3 clean greased and floured 2-pound cans or 1 greased and floured
bundt pan. Bake at 325 degrees for 1¼ hours. Cool in the cans on a wire rack
for 10 minutes. Remove to a wire rack to cool completely. Add enough milk to the confectioners'
sugar in a bowl to make of glaze consistency and mix well. Drizzle over the cakes, allowing the
glaze to run down the side to resemble burning candles. While the glaze is still soft, garnish
with a red cherry in the center and green cherries cut to resemble leaves.
Yield: 16 servings
Maria Motta

MIAMI BEACH BIRTHDAY CAKE

½ cup graham cracker crumbs
⅓ cup melted butter
½ cup chopped pecans or walnuts
⅔ cup miniature chocolate chips
2 cups flour, sifted
1 teaspoon baking soda
1 teaspoon salt
½ cup butter, softened
1½ cups sugar
2 eggs
⅓ cup melted miniature chocolate chips
1 teaspoon vanilla extract
1½ cups buttermilk or sour milk
1 cup whipping cream
2 tablespoons sugar

Mix the graham cracker crumbs with the melted butter in a bowl. Stir in the pecans and ⅔ cup chocolate chips. Set aside. Mix the flour, baking soda and salt together and set aside. Cream ½ cup butter in a mixer bowl. Add 1½ cups sugar gradually, beating constantly until light and fluffy. Beat in the eggs 1 at a time. Blend in the melted chocolate and vanilla. Add the flour mixture and milk alternately to the creamed mixture, beginning and ending with the flour mixture. Beat well at low speed after each addition. Pour the batter into 2 greased and floured 9-inch cake pans. Sprinkle with the crumb mixture. Bake at 350 degrees for 30 to 40 minutes or until the layers test done. Let cool. Whip the cream with 2 tablespoons sugar in a mixer bowl. Spread between the layers and over the top and side of the cake. Chill until serving time.

Yield: 12 servings

Claudia A. Soares

Orange Rum Savarin

1 envelope active dry yeast
3 tablespoons sugar
⅓ cup very warm water
4 eggs, at room temperature
3 cups sifted flour

⅔ cup butter, softened
Rum Syrup
½ cup apricot or peach
preserves, melted

Sprinkle the yeast and a very small amount of the sugar over the warm water in a large mixer bowl, stirring to dissolve. Let stand for 10 minutes or until bubbly. Add the remaining sugar, eggs and 2 cups of the flour. Beat for 2 minutes. Beat in the butter 1 tablespoon at a time. Stir in the remaining 1 cup flour. Cover and let rise in a warm place until doubled in bulk. Stir the dough down. Turn into a buttered 8-cup brioche pan or ovenproof bowl. Let rise in a warm place until doubled in bulk. Bake at 375 degrees for 50 minutes or until the cake sounds hollow when tapped. Remove to a wire rack to cool. Place the cake on a deep platter. Baste with hot rum syrup, allowing the cake to absorb the syrup. Brush with the preserves. Garnish with ⅓ cup chopped candied orange peel, marzipan or maraschino cherries. Decorate with holly leaves if desired.
Yield: 12 servings

Anne M. Brady

RUM SYRUP

2 cups orange juice
1½ cups sugar

¾ cup light rum

Combine the orange juice and sugar in a large saucepan. Simmer for 15 minutes. Remove from the heat. Stir in the rum.

FRUIT-FILLED COOKIE BOATS FOR THE JEWISH HOLIDAYS

1½ cups matzo meal
1 cup potato flour
⅛ teaspoon salt
½ cup shortening
1 cup sugar
4 eggs
2 tablespoons lemon juice
1 teaspoon grated lemon peel
1 cup dried pitted prunes
1 cup dried apricots
1 small lemon, sliced
1 cup sugar

Sift the meal, flour and salt together. Cream the shortening and 1 cup sugar in a mixer bowl until light and fluffy. Beat in the eggs 1 at a time. Add the lemon juice and peel and mix well. Add the flour mixture to the creamed mixture and mix well. Let stand for 1 hour or until thickened. Combine the prunes, apricots and lemon with water to cover in a saucepan. Bring to a boil. Simmer for 20 minutes or until the fruit is tender. Add 1 cup sugar, stirring until dissolved; drain, reserving the juice for another use. Let the fruit cool. Chop the fruit together. Drop rounded tablespoonfuls of batter onto a greased cookie sheet, shaping into oblongs. Make an indentation in each cookie with your thumb so that the cookie resembles a boat. Spoon the fruit mixture into the indentations. Bake at 400 degrees for 12 to 15 minutes or until brown. Store in airtight containers for up to 2 weeks.

Yield: 2½ dozen

Rachel Castino

CHRISTMAS COOKIES

½ teaspoon baking soda
1 teaspoon vinegar
1 pound butter, softened
2½ cups sugar

2 eggs
5 cups flour
1 egg white
Jimmies

Dissolve the baking soda in the vinegar. Cream the butter and sugar in a mixer bowl. Add the eggs, beating until light and fluffy. Add the baking soda mixture and flour and mix well. Chill for 1 hour. Roll the dough as thin as possible on a floured surface. Cut with cookie cutters. Place on a nonstick cookie sheet. Brush with the egg white. Sprinkle with jimmies. Bake at 400 degrees until the edges are slightly brown. Watch carefully because these cookies bake quickly.

Yield: 4 to 5 dozen

Debra Ladd

OATMEAL DROP LEFRANCOIS COOKIES

1½ cups flour
½ teaspoon salt
½ teaspoon baking soda
1 teaspoon ginger
1 teaspoon cinnamon
1 teaspoon nutmeg
1½ cups rolled oats

1 cup sugar
½ cup melted shortening
1 egg, beaten
½ cup milk
½ cup chopped walnuts
1 cup raisins

Sift the flour, salt, baking soda, ginger, cinnamon and nutmeg together. Mix the oats, sugar and shortening in a bowl. Add the egg and milk and mix well. Add the flour mixture and mix well. Stir in the walnuts and raisins. Drop by heaping teaspoonfuls onto a cookie sheet. Bake at 350 degrees for 15 minutes or until brown.

Yield: 1½ to 2 dozen

Debra Raymond

KAHLÚA FUDGE BROWNIES

1½ cups flour
½ teaspoon baking powder
½ teaspoon salt
⅔ cup butter
3 ounces semisweet chocolate

3 eggs
2 cups sugar
¾ cup chopped walnuts (optional)
¼ cup plus 1 tablespoon Kahlúa

Sift the flour, baking powder and salt together. Melt the butter and chocolate in a saucepan over low heat, stirring frequently. Beat the eggs and sugar in a mixer bowl until light. Add the flour mixture, chocolate mixture, walnuts and ¼ cup of the Kahlúa and mix well. Pour into a foil-lined greased 9x9-inch baking pan. Bake at 350 degrees for 30 minutes or until the top springs back when lightly touched and the edges begin to pull away from the sides of the pan. Cool in the pan. Brush with the remaining 1 tablespoon Kahlúa.
Cut into squares
Yield: 8 to 10 servings
Michelle Baptiste

CRANBERRY PIE

1½ cups whole cranberries
¼ cup packed brown sugar
¼ cup chopped walnuts
1 egg

½ cup sugar
½ cup flour
⅓ cup melted butter

Place the cranberries in a greased 9-inch glass pie plate. Sprinkle with the brown sugar and walnuts. Beat the egg and sugar in a medium bowl. Add the flour and butter and mix well. Pour over the cranberries. Bake at 325 degrees for 45 minutes.
Serve warm with vanilla ice cream.
Yield: 6 servings
Sophie Pelletier

CRANBERRY MOUSSE

1 cup cranberry juice
1 (3-ounce) package
   raspberry gelatin

1 (16-ounce) can cranberry sauce
2 cups whipped topping

Bring the cranberry juice to a boil in a saucepan; remove from the heat. Stir in the gelatin until dissolved. Beat the cranberry sauce at high speed in a mixer bowl. Stir in the gelatin mixture. Pour into a decorative bowl. Chill for 2½ hours or until thickened. Fold in the whipped topping. Chill for several hours or until thickened and firm.

Yield: 8 servings

Alice LaBelle

SINFUL FRENCH SILK PIE

1 cup margarine, softened
1⅓ cups sugar
5 ounces unsweetened chocolate,
   melted, cooled
1 tablespoon Grand
Marnier orange-flavor liqueur

4 eggs
1 baked (9-inch) deep-dish pie
shell, or 1 baked (10-inch) pie shell
1 cup whipping cream, whipped
1 ounce semisweet chocolate,
   shaved

Cream the margarine and sugar in a mixer bowl until light and fluffy. Add the chocolate and liqueur and mix well. Add 2 of the eggs. Beat for 5 minutes; do not underbeat. Add the remaining 2 eggs. Beat for 5 minutes longer; do not underbeat. Spread in the pie shell. Chill for 2 to 3 hours or until set. Top with the whipped cream and chocolate shavings.

Yield: 6 to 8 servings

Jeanine Y. Sasseville

SOMBRERO PIE

24 Oreo cookies, crushed
¼ cup melted butter
1 (16-ounce) jar marshmallow
creme

½ cup Kahlúa
2 cups whipping cream, whipped

Set aside ¼ cup of the cookie crumbs. Mix the remaining crumbs with the butter. Press into a 9-inch pie plate. Mix the marshmallow creme and Kahlúa in a bowl. Add the whipped cream and mix gently. Spoon into the pie plate. Freeze for 2 to 3 hours or until firm. Let stand for 5 minutes before slicing. Sprinkle with the reserved crumbs.
Yield: 6 to 8 servings
Paula Benedetti

STRAWBERRY CREAM PIE

¾ cup hot water
1 (3-ounce) package strawberry
gelatin
2 cups whipping cream, whipped

1½ cups sliced fresh strawberries
or 10 ounces frozen strawberries
1 baked (9-inch) pie shell or
graham cracker pie shell

Pour the hot water over the gelatin in a small bowl. Stir with a wooden spoon until the gelatin is dissolved. Chill for 20 minutes or until partially set. Fold the whipped cream into the gelatin. Stir in the strawberries. Pour into the pie shell. Chill for 1 to 2 hours or until set.
Yield: 6 to 8 servings
Beth Gissinger

CRÈME DE MENTHE
CHOCOLATE CHEESECAKE

2 cups chocolate wafer crumbs
¼ cup melted butter
¼ teaspoon cinnamon
32 ounces cream cheese, softened
1½ cups sugar
4 eggs
2¾ tablespoons green crème de menthe
½ teaspoon peppermint extract
¼ teaspoon salt
½ cup semisweet chocolate chips or mint chocolate chips
1 cup whipping cream, whipped

Combine the cookie crumbs, butter and cinnamon in a large bowl and mix well. Press over the bottom of a greased and floured 9-inch springform pan. Blend the cream cheese and sugar in a large mixer bowl. Add the eggs and beat until smooth. Add the crème de menthe, peppermint flavoring and salt and beat well. Pour into the prepared pan. Add the chocolate chips, stirring gently just until mixed. Bake at 325 degrees for 45 minutes. Turn off the oven. Let the cheesecake stand in the closed oven for 1 hour. Chill until serving time. Remove the side of the pan. Transfer carefully to a platter. Top with the whipped cream.

Yield: 16 servings

Nancy Edwards

Pumpkin Cheesecake

¼ cup graham cracker crumbs
32 ounces cream cheese, softened
1½ cups sugar
5 eggs
¼ cup flour
¼ teaspoon salt
1 pound pumpkin, cooked, mashed
2 teaspoons pumpkin pie spice

Butter the side and bottom of a springform pan. Sprinkle the graham cracker crumbs in the pan. Beat the cream cheese in a mixer bowl until fluffy. Add the sugar gradually, beating constantly. Beat in the eggs 1 at a time. Add the flour, salt, pumpkin and spice and mix well. Pour into the prepared pan. Bake at 325 degrees for 1½ hours or until the edge of the cheesecake is firm but the center is still soft. Turn off the oven. Let the cheesecake stand with the oven door open for 30 minutes. Remove the side from the pan.

Yield: 10 servings

Elizabeth Souza

WHITE CHOCOLATE
AMARETTO CHEESECAKE

1 cup graham cracker crumbs
¾ cup amaretti macaroon crumbs
3 tablespoons sugar
½ cup melted unsalted butter
1 pound white chocolate
½ cup sugar
1½ pounds cream cheese, softened
¼ cup amaretto
⅛ teaspoon almond extract
4 eggs
1 cup whole milk yogurt
8 to 10 candied violets

Mix the graham cracker crumbs, cookie crumbs, 3 tablespoons sugar and butter in a bowl. Press into a buttered 9-inch springform pan. Melt the white chocolate in a double boiler over simmering water. Let cool. Cream ½ cup sugar and cream cheese in a mixer bowl. Beat in the amaretto and almond extract. Beat in the eggs 1 at a time. Beat in the chocolate. Add the yogurt, beating at low speed just until mixed; do not overbeat. Pour into the prepared pan. Place the springform pan in a larger baking pan. Pour hot water around the springform pan. Bake at 375 degrees for 1¼ hours or until set. Let stand on a wire rack for 15 minutes before removing the side of the pan. Cool completely. Decorate with the candied violets. Chill for 4 to 6 hours.

Yield: 8 to 10 servings

Margo J. Moore

CASHEW NUT CHOCOLATE MOUSSE

2 ounces unsweetened chocolate,
  broken into small pieces
½ cup sugar
5 egg yolks

1 cup finely ground
  toasted cashews
1 cup whipping cream, whipped
5 egg whites, stiffly beaten

Heat the chocolate and sugar in a double boiler over hot water until the chocolate is melted and the sugar is dissolved, stirring constantly. Remove from the heat. Beat in the egg yolks 1 at a time. Stir in the cashews. Fold in the whipped cream and egg whites. Pour into a 1-quart soufflé dish. Chill for several hours to overnight. Serve with sweetened whipped cream.

Yield: 6 to 8 servings

Mrs. John A. Pannoni

COCONUT ALMOND CUSTARD

½ cup sugar
½ cup water
1 (3-inch) cinnamon stick,
  broken into pieces
4 ounces flaked coconut

3 cups whole milk
4 eggs
¼ teaspoon almond extract
½ cup whipping cream, whipped
2 tablespoons toasted almonds

Combine the sugar, water and cinnamon in a large saucepan. Simmer for 10 minutes. Strain and discard the cinnamon pieces. Add the coconut to the sugar mixture. Simmer for 5 minutes, stirring frequently. Stir in 2½ cups of the milk. Cook until hot, stirring constantly. Beat the eggs with the remaining ½ cup milk in a bowl. Stir 1 cup of the hot mixture into the eggs; stir the eggs into the hot mixture. Cook until thickened, stirring constantly; do not boil. Stir in the flavoring. Pour into a 1½-quart bowl. Chill thoroughly. Mound the whipped cream in the center of the custard. Top with the almonds.

Yield: 8 servings

Gloria Homer

GRAPE-NUT CUSTARD PUDDING

6 eggs
1 cup sugar
¼ teaspoon salt
1 quart milk

1 teaspoon vanilla extract
¾ cup Grape-Nuts
Nutmeg to taste

Beat the eggs in a mixer bowl. Add the sugar and salt and mix well. Add the milk and vanilla and mix well. Pour into a greased 9x13-inch baking pan. Sprinkle with the Grape-Nuts and nutmeg. Bake at 400 degrees for 30 minutes.

Yield: 12 to 15 servings

Violette Robert

TIA YIA'S GREEK CUSTARD

1 quart milk
¾ cup sugar
¾ cup farina
¼ teaspoon salt

½ cup margarine
4 eggs, lightly beaten
Cinnamon to taste

Scald the milk in a medium saucepan. Add the sugar, farina and salt. Cook over low heat until thickened, stirring constantly. Remove from the heat. Add the margarine and eggs gradually and mix well. Pour into a greased 9x13-inch baking pan. Sprinkle with cinnamon. Bake at 350 degrees for 45 to 60 minutes or until golden brown. Let cool. Cut into squares.

Note: This custard is perishable and should be refrigerated when cool.

Yield: 12 to 15 servings

Tina Gaudette

LEMON CLOUD PIE

1 package lemon pudding and
pie filling mix
3 ounces cream cheese, softened

¼ cup sugar
2 egg whites
Whipped topping

Cook the pie filling mix according to the package directions. Let cool. Combine the pie filling and cream cheese in a bowl and mix well. Beat the sugar and egg whites in a mixer bowl. Fold into the cream cheese mixture. Let cool. Top with the whipped topping.

Yield: 4 to 6 servings

Yvonne Mello

VANESSA'S PINEAPPLE DESSERT

1 (1-layer) package yellow
cake mix
1 small package vanilla instant
pudding mix
1½ cups milk
8 ounces cream cheese, softened

1 (16- to 20-ounce) can crushed
pineapple, drained
16 ounces whipped topping
½ cup chopped walnuts (optional)
1 (10-ounce) jar cherries

Prepare and bake the cake mix using the package directions for a 9x13-inch cake pan. Let cool for 20 to 25 minutes. Mix the pudding mix and milk in a bowl. Blend in the cream cheese. Spread over the baked layer. Spread the pineapple over the pudding. Top with the whipped topping. Sprinkle with the walnuts and cherries. Chill until serving time.

Yield: 12 to 15 servings

Laura De Motta

CRANBERRY SQUARES

1 cup margarine
1½ cups sugar
1½ cups flour

2 eggs, beaten
2 cups whole cranberries
¾ cup chopped walnuts or pecans

Melt the margarine in a large saucepan. Remove from the heat. Stir in the sugar and flour. Add the eggs and mix well. Stir in the cranberries and walnuts. Pour into a greased 9x13-inch baking pan. Bake at 325 degrees for 40 to 45 minutes or until set. Cut into squares to serve.

Yield: 12 to 15 servings

Yvonne Mello

FRUIT PUNCH BARS

2 eggs
1½ cups sugar
1 (17-ounce) can fruit cocktail
2¼ cups flour
1½ teaspoons baking powder
½ teaspoon salt
1 teaspoon vanilla extract

1⅓ cups flaked coconut
½ cup chopped walnuts
¾ cup sugar
½ cup butter
¼ cup evaporated milk
½ teaspoon vanilla extract
½ cup chopped walnuts

Beat the eggs and 1½ cups sugar at high speed in a large mixer bowl until light and fluffy. Add the undrained fruit cocktail, flour, baking powder, salt and 1 teaspoon vanilla. Beat at medium speed until blended, scraping the side and bottom of the bowl occasionally. Spread in a greased and floured 10x15-inch baking pan. Sprinkle with the coconut and ½ cup walnuts. Bake at 350 degrees for 20 to 25 minutes or until golden brown. Combine ¾ cup sugar, butter, evaporated milk and ½ teaspoon vanilla in a small saucepan. Bring to a boil. Boil for 2 minutes, stirring constantly. Remove from the heat. Stir in ½ cup walnuts. Let cool. Drizzle over the hot dessert. Cut into bars.

Yield: 24 servings

Mary Souza

MAZUREK
(POLISH DESSERT SQUARES)

1½ cups flour
1 cup sugar
¼ teaspoon salt
1 cup butter, softened
6 egg yolks
¼ cup finely chopped almonds

2 tablespoons medium cream
1 cup sugar
1 egg
Juice and grated zest of 1 lemon
½ cup finely chopped almonds

Sift the flour, 1 cup sugar and salt together. Beat the butter in a mixer bowl. Add the flour mixture and 1 egg yolk at a time alternately, mixing well after each addition. Stir in ¼ cup almonds and cream. Pour into a greased 10x15-inch baking pan. Bake at 350 degrees for 30 minutes. Beat 1 cup sugar, 1 egg, lemon juice and lemon zest in a mixer bowl until thick. Add ½ cup almonds. Spread over the pastry. Bake for 10 minutes or until golden brown. Cool and cut into squares. Store in an airtight container.
Yield: 24 servings
Margaret Ponte

BANANAS FOSTER

¼ cup butter or margarine
½ cup packed light brown sugar
4 ripe bananas, peeled, cut into
halves lengthwise
⅛ teaspoon cinnamon

½ cup light rum
¼ cup crème de bananas
(banana liqueur)
1 pint vanilla ice cream, or 1 cup
sweetened whipped cream

Melt the butter and brown sugar in a flat chafing dish or attractive skillet. Add the bananas in a single layer. Sauté for 5 minutes or until tender, turning once. Sprinkle with cinnamon. Pour in the rum and liqueur. Ignite with a match; remove from the heat. Baste the bananas with the cooking liquid until the flame subsides. Serve immediately with the ice cream or whipped cream.
Yield: 4 servings
Madeline M. Quintal

CHOCOLATE ECLAIR CAKE

1 package graham crackers
3½ cups milk
2 (4-ounce) packages vanilla instant pudding mix
8 ounces whipped topping
2 ounces unsweetened chocolate
2 teaspoons light corn syrup
1 teaspoon vanilla extract
1½ cups confectioners' sugar
3 tablespoons butter
3 tablespoons milk

Line a 9x13-inch pan with some of the graham crackers. Beat the milk and pudding mix in a mixer bowl until thick. Fold in the whipped topping. Spread half the mixture over the graham crackers. Add layers of half the remaining graham crackers, remaining pudding mixture and remaining graham crackers. Melt the chocolate in a saucepan over low heat, stirring constantly. Add the corn syrup, vanilla, confectioners' sugar, butter and milk. Cook for 3 to 4 minutes or until smooth, stirring constantly. Pour the chocolate over the top layer of graham crackers. Spread to cover all the graham crackers. Chill for 48 hours.

Yield: 12 servings

Kathy Kendrigan

Cinnamon Fruit Biscuit Crunches

1 (10-count) can refrigerator
biscuits
¼ cup melted margarine or butter
½ cup sugar

½ teaspoon cinnamon
10 teaspoons plum, strawberry or
other preserves

Separate the dough into 10 biscuits. Dip both sides of the biscuits in the melted margarine, then in a mixture of the sugar and cinnamon. Make a deep indentation with your thumb in the center of each biscuit. Fill each with 1 teaspoon of the preserves. Place in a baking pan. Bake at 375 degrees for 15 to 20 minutes or until golden brown.

Yield: 10 servings

Cathy Wolfe

Fresh Fruit Amaretti

1 small can mandarin oranges
2 tablespoons lemon juice
3 medium pears, cored, diced
2 to 3 bananas, sliced
1½ cups coarsely crushed
macaroons

5 kiwifruit, peeled, sliced,
cut into halves
1½ cups seedless red or green
grapes
16 ounces vanilla yogurt
1 cup sour cream

Drain the oranges, reserving the juice. Mix the orange juice and lemon juice in a bowl. Dip the pear and banana slices in the mixture to prevent the fruit from becoming brown. Sprinkle ¾ cup of the crumbs in a 2-quart bowl. Arrange half the pears, kiwifruit and grapes over the crumbs. Mix the yogurt and sour cream in a bowl. Spoon half the mixture over the fruit in the bowl. Repeat the layers. Top with the oranges and bananas. Chill, covered, for 1 hour. Note: Any fruit can be used in this recipe.

Yield: 8 to 10 servings

Rose Trahan

FRUITED CLOUDS

2 cups sour cream
⅔ cup sugar
4 ounces whipped topping
¾ to 1 cup milk
1 (17-ounce) can fruit cocktail, drained
1 can pineapple chunks, drained
1 can mandarin oranges or tangerines
¾ cup colored miniature marshmallows
½ cup dried coconut
½ cup chopped pecans or walnuts

Whip the sour cream by hand in a large mixer bowl. Add the sugar and whip by hand
or with a mixer until smooth. Add the whipped topping and mix well. Beat in enough
milk to make of a thick but not stiff consistency. Fold in the fruit cocktail,
pineapple and mandarin oranges. Add the marshmallows, coconut and pecans and mix well.
Pour into dessert dishes. Garnish with additional coconut, nuts and cherries. Chill for 5 minutes
before serving. Note: This dessert is very versatile. You may replace the canned fruit with 2
medium peeled and diced apples, 2 peeled and diced pears, seedless grapes, 1 banana and
2 diced peaches. You may add any fruit that is in season or that suits your personal
preferences, such as melon, pitted fresh cherries, watermelon, fresh pineapple and mango.
Yield: 8 servings

Mrs. Sudarshan K. Ishrish

FRESH FRUIT CRISP

6 cups peeled sliced tart apples or pears
2 tablespoons lemon juice
$\frac{1}{4}$ cup sugar or honey
2 tablespoons melted butter or margarine
$\frac{1}{4}$ teaspoon salt
1 teaspoon cinnamon
3 tablespoons butter or margarine, softened
$\frac{1}{3}$ cup sugar
1 tablespoon flour
1$\frac{1}{2}$ cups bran flakes or other flaked cereal

Combine the apples, lemon juice, $\frac{1}{4}$ cup sugar, 2 tablespoons butter, salt and cinnamon in a bowl and mix well. Spoon into an 8-inch round baking dish or a shallow 1$\frac{1}{2}$-quart baking dish. Beat 3 tablespoons butter in a mixer bowl. Blend in $\frac{1}{3}$ cup sugar and flour. Stir in the cereal. Sprinkle over the apple mixture. Bake, covered, at 375 degrees for 15 minutes. Bake, uncovered, for 15 minutes longer or until the apples are tender. Serve warm with whipped topping, whipped cream or ice cream.

Yield: 6 to 8 servings

Peggy Gross

Parisian Mocha Cream Loaf

1½ cups cake flour
⅔ cup milk
¼ cup shortening
1¼ teaspoons baking powder
½ teaspoon salt
½ teaspoon almond extract
1 egg
¾ cup sugar
1½ cups whipping cream or heavy cream
1 tablespoon baking cocoa
1 tablespoon instant espresso powder
1 tablespoon sugar
2 tablespoons apricot preserves

Combine the flour, milk, shortening, baking powder, salt, almond flavoring, egg and ¾ cup sugar in a large bowl. Beat at low speed until mixed, scraping the side of the bowl constantly with a plastic spatula. Increase the speed to medium. Beat for 3 minutes or until light and fluffy. Spread the batter evenly in a greased and floured 9x12-inch baking pan. Bake at 375 degrees for 20 minutes or until the top is golden brown and a wooden pick inserted near the center comes out clean. Cool on a wire rack for 10 minutes. Remove to a wire rack to cool completely. Beat ½ cup of the whipping cream at medium speed in a small mixer bowl until soft peaks form. Spoon into a decorator tube fitted with a medium rosette tip. Place in the refrigerator until needed. For the mocha cream, beat the remaining whipping cream, cocoa, espresso powder and 1 tablespoon sugar in a small mixer bowl until soft peaks form. Cut the cake crosswise into thirds with a serrated knife. Place 1 layer on a plate. Spread the cake layer with ½ cup of the mocha cream. Repeat the process with the remaining 2 layers. Pipe the whipped cream in the decorator tube into 1-inch diamond shapes on the top of the cake. Fill alternate diamonds with the preserves.

Yield: 12 servings

Michele Maciel

Strawberry Scrumptious

1½ cups finely crushed
vanilla wafers
2 tablespoons sugar
¼ cup melted butter or margarine
4 egg whites

½ cup sugar
1 pint fresh strawberries, sliced
¼ cup sugar
1 cup whipping cream, whipped

Mix the cookie crumbs, 2 tablespoons sugar and butter in an 8x8-inch baking pan. Press evenly over the bottom of the pan. Beat the egg whites in a large mixer bowl until soft peaks form. Add ½ cup sugar gradually, beating constantly until stiff peaks form. Spread the meringue over the crumb mixture. Bake at 350 degrees for 15 minutes. Let cool. Sprinkle the strawberries with ¼ cup sugar. Let stand for 10 to 15 minutes; drain. Spread the whipped cream over the meringue. Top with the strawberries. Chill until serving time.
Yield: 8 to 10 servings
Lynne McGrath

German Nut Bread

1 cup melted butter or margarine
2 cups sugar
4 eggs, lightly beaten
1 teaspoon baking powder
2 cups flour

1 cup sour cream
1 teaspoon vanilla extract
2 cups chopped walnuts
1 (10-ounce) jar cherries, drained

Mix the butter and sugar in a large bowl. Add the eggs, baking powder and flour and mix well. Fold in the sour cream, vanilla, walnuts and cherries. Pour into a greased bundt pan. Bake at 350 degrees for 1 hour. Let cool for 10 minutes.
Yield: 16 servings
Claire Gonsalves

Double-Quick Cherry Butterscotch Coffee Bread

⅓ cup butter
½ cup brown sugar
1 tablespoon corn syrup
½ cup walnut halves
½ cup maraschino cherries
1 envelope active dry yeast
¾ cup warm water
¼ cup sugar
1 teaspoon salt
2¼ cups sifted flour
1 egg
¼ cup shortening

Combine the butter, brown sugar and corn syrup in a 9-inch ring mold. Heat until the butter is melted and the brown sugar is dissolved. Arrange the walnuts and cherries alternately on the bottom of the mold. Let cool to lukewarm. Dissolve the yeast in the warm water. Add the sugar, salt and half the flour and beat well. Add the egg, shortening and remaining flour gradually, beating until smooth. Drop by small spoonfuls into the prepared mold, being sure to cover the bottom of the mold. Let rise, covered, in a warm place for 50 to 60 minutes or until the dough is slightly above the top of the mold. Bake at 375 degrees for 30 to 35 minutes or until brown. Invert immediately onto a plate to avoid sticking.

Yield: 8 to 10 servings

Pat Schweidenback

ORANGE STREUSEL MUFFINS

2 cups flour
½ cup chopped pecans
⅓ cup sugar
1 tablespoon baking powder
½ teaspoon salt
½ cup orange juice
½ cup orange marmalade
¼ cup milk
¼ cup vegetable oil
1 tablespoon grated orange peel
1 egg, lightly beaten
¼ cup sugar
1 tablespoon flour
½ teaspoon cinnamon
¼ teaspoon nutmeg
1 tablespoon butter or margarine, softened

Combine 2 cups flour, pecans, ⅓ cup sugar, baking powder and salt in a large bowl
and mix well. Combine the orange juice, marmalade, milk, oil, orange peel and egg in a medium
bowl and mix well. Add the marmalade mixture to the flour mixture, stirring just until
moistened. Fill paper-lined muffin cups ¾ full with the batter. Combine ¼ cup sugar,
1 tablespoon flour, cinnamon, nutmeg and butter in a small bowl and mix well.
Sprinkle evenly over the batter. Bake at 400 degrees for 20 to 25 minutes or until
a wooden pick inserted near the center comes out clean. Serve warm.
Yield: 1 dozen

Patricia Grochmal

ZESTY LEMON MUFFINS

2 cups flour
2 teaspoons baking powder
½ teaspoon salt
2 teaspoons poppy seeds
½ cup butter, softened
½ cup sugar

2 eggs
½ cup milk
1 tablespoon grated lemon peel
3 tablespoons fresh lemon juice
5 tablespoons sugar

Sift the flour, baking powder and salt together. Add the poppy seeds. Cream the butter and ½ cup sugar in a mixer bowl until light and fluffy. Beat in the eggs 1 at a time. Add the flour mixture, milk and lemon peel alternately, beating well after each addition. Pour into large nonstick muffin cups. Bake at 375 degrees for 20 to 25 minutes or until the muffins test done. Heat the lemon juice and 5 tablespoons sugar in a saucepan, stirring until the sugar dissolves; do not boil. Dip the tops of the muffins into the lemon juice mixture.

Yield: 1 dozen

Kathy Reed

DIET PINEAPPLE DESSERT

1 package lime gelatin
1 cup hot water
3 ounces cream cheese, softened

1 cup crushed pineapple, drained
1 can diet lemon-lime soda

Dissolve the gelatin in the hot water in a mixer bowl. Beat in the cream cheese. Add the pineapple and soda. Chill until set. May serve with a dollop of whipped topping.

Yield: 4 to 6 servings

Juanita Jones

From Our Local Restaurants

Butler Flats Lighthouse

Butler Flats lighthouse was built in 1898 and is located in New Bedford Harbor. It was manned by five enlisted men and two officers who maintained the light and fog signal until 1975.

The unique feature of this lighthouse is that the tower above the cast-iron caisson is constructed primarily of brick.

CHICKEN AND SHRIMP IMPERIAL

1½ pounds boneless chicken breasts
½ cup flour
Salt and pepper to taste
¼ cup vegetable oil
¼ cup butter
1 pound small shrimp, peeled, deveined
2 tablespoons chopped shallots
½ cup white wine
¾ cup brown gravy (optional)
2 cups whipping cream
4 teaspoons whole grain mustard
1 teaspoon mustard

Rinse the chicken and pat dry. Mix the flour, salt and pepper in a shallow dish. Dredge the chicken in the mixture. Heat the oil and butter in a large skillet until the butter melts. Add the chicken. Cook until light brown on both sides. Cook over low heat for 5 minutes longer or until the chicken is cooked through. Add the shrimp. Cook for 3 to 4 minutes or until the shrimp turn pink. Remove the chicken and shrimp to a serving platter. Cook the shallots in the skillet until light brown. Add the wine to deglaze the skillet. Add the gravy, cream, whole grain mustard and mustard. Simmer until of the desired sauce consistency. Adjust the seasonings. Pour the sauce over the chicken and shrimp. Garnish with freshly chopped parsley. Serve with rice pilaf.
Yield: 4 servings

Blue Point Restaurant

BAKED FINNAN HADDIE WITH CREAM SAUCE

¾ to 1 pound finnan haddie
(smoked haddock)
1 cup milk

Cream Sauce
1 small onion, sliced

Place the fish skin side down in a shallow dish. Cover with the milk. Soak the fish overnight in the refrigerator; drain. Remove the skin from the fish. Place the fish in a greased ovenproof pan. Cover with cream sauce. Top with the onion. Bake at 350 degrees for 30 to 35 minutes or until the fish is cooked through. Serve on toast points or mashed potatoes. Garnish with a chopped hard-cooked egg and chopped parsley.
Yield: 2 servings

Fairhaven Chowder House

CREAM SAUCE

2 tablespoons butter
(not margarine)
2 tablespoons flour
1 cup milk

⅛ teaspoon ground cloves, or
to taste
1 bay leaf
⅛ teaspoon salt, or to taste

Melt the butter in a saucepan over low heat. Add the flour. Cook for 3 to 4 minutes or until heated through, stirring constantly. Blend in the milk gradually. Add the cloves, bay leaf and salt. Cook for 4 to 5 minutes or until thick and smooth, stirring constantly. Remove the bay leaf.

FREESTONE'S CITY GRILL ALPHABET SOUP

1 (23-ounce) can tomatoes
1 pound ground beef
½ medium onion, chopped
4 cups water
3 beef bouillon cubes
2 carrots, sliced
2 ribs celery, sliced
1 teaspoon salt
1 teaspoon Worcestershire sauce
1 clove of garlic, chopped
½ teaspoon pepper
2 tablespoons chopped parsley
4 servings cooked alphabet pasta or other small pasta

Purée the tomatoes lightly in a blender and set aside. Brown the ground beef in a large saucepan, stirring until crumbly; drain. Add the tomatoes, onion, water, bouillon cubes, carrots, celery, salt, Worcestershire sauce, garlic, pepper and parsley and mix well. Bring to a boil. Simmer, covered, for 1 hour. Stir in the pasta.

Yield: 4 servings

Freestone's City Grill

HAM AND APPLE PIE

1 recipe (2-crust) pie pastry (see Note)
8 to 10 Granny Smith apples, peeled, sliced
2 tablespoons flour
½ cup packed brown sugar
Cinnamon, nutmeg, cloves and white pepper to taste
1 pound cooked ham, julienned
1 to 2 tablespoons butter
2 egg yolks
¾ cup (about) whipping cream
Melted Cheddar cheese

Fit 1 pastry into a pie plate. Combine the apples, flour, brown sugar, cinnamon, nutmeg, cloves and pepper in a bowl and mix well. Add the ham. Pour into the pastry-lined pie plate. Dot with the butter. Top with the remaining pastry. Cut numerous slits in the top pastry. Make a thumb-sized hole in the center of the pastry. Place 2 egg yolks in a 2-cup measure. Add enough cream to measure 1 cup. Mix with a wire whisk. Pour through the hole in the pastry. Bake at 350 degrees for 1 hour or until the crust is golden brown and the apples are tender. Let stand for 20 minutes or longer before serving. Top each serving with cheese.

Note: If making pie pastry is a problem, try making a deep-dish pie, using just a top crust of crescent roll dough or even biscuits.

Yield: 6 to 8 servings

Mattapoisett Inn

POTATO CHEESE PANCAKES

2½ tablespoons flour
7 ounces cream cheese, softened
1½ cups shredded Swiss cheese
½ cup whipping cream
2 eggs, beaten
½ teaspoon salt
⅛ to ¼ teaspoon cayenne, or to taste
¼ teaspoon garlic powder
Grated potatoes (see Note)
Bacon drippings

Mix the flour and cream cheese in a medium bowl. Combine the Swiss cheese, cream, eggs, salt, cayenne and garlic powder in a large bowl. Add the flour mixture and mix well. Add enough potatoes to make of the desired consistency and mix well. Shape into patties. Dredge in the flour mixture. Heat the bacon drippings in a large skillet. Add the patties. Fry until cooked through and golden brown. Note: If new potatoes (the kind with the smooth, thin skin) are in season, there is no need to peel them. Grated potatoes should be dried to remove excess moisture; they should be stirred in quickly and cooked immediately or they will blacken. They can be kept warm in the oven during the frying.

Yield: 4 to 6 servings

Mattapoisett Inn

SPAGHETTINI WITH LITTLENECKS, LEEKS, SAFFRON AND MARJORAM

1 medium leek
6 tablespoons virgin olive oil
½ tablespoon saffron threads
2 cloves of garlic, chopped
½ cup chopped flat-leaf Italian parsley
24 littleneck clams
1½ cups dry white wine
¼ cup chopped fresh marjoram leaves
Salt and pepper to taste
4 servings cooked spaghettini

Cut the leek into ⅛-inch julienne strips. Sauté the leek in the olive oil in a stockpot over medium heat until soft but not brown. Add the saffron. Cook until the saffron is broken up. Add the garlic and parsley. Add the littlenecks and wine. Cover and bring to a boil. Boil until all the littlenecks have opened. Stir in the marjoram. Season with salt and pepper. Pour the pasta into a large serving bowl. Add all the liquid from cooking the littlenecks and mix well. Arrange the littlenecks over the pasta. Serve immediately.

Yield: 4 servings

The Pasta House

PASTA PUTTANESCA

1 can tomato sauce
1 can peeled diced tomatoes
2 teaspoons minced garlic
1 tablespoon olive oil
1 teaspoon dried basil
2 teaspoons Antonio's hot chopped red peppers
⅛ teaspoon black pepper, or to taste
1 cup pitted black olives, cut into halves lengthwise
¾ cup pimento-stuffed green olives, sliced
2 tablespoons capers, drained
1 pound vermicelli, cooked
Grated Parmesan cheese (optional)

Combine the tomato sauce, tomatoes, garlic, olive oil, basil, red peppers and black pepper in a large saucepan and mix well. Cook over medium heat until hot; reduce the heat. Add the black olives, green olives and capers. Simmer, covered, over very low heat for 5 to 10 minutes or until the flavors are blended. Pour over the hot pasta. Sprinkle with cheese.

Yield: 4 servings

Riccardi's

BRAISED CHICKEN WITH ONIONS, TOMATOES, MUSHROOMS AND RED WINE

2 cups chopped mushrooms
4 to 6 shallots, roasted, chopped
2 large onions, chopped, or several pearl onions
2 leeks, chopped
1 carrot, chopped
4 to 6 tomatoes, peeled, chopped
1 tablespoon olive oil
3 pounds boneless chicken, lightly browned
1 cup red wine
¼ cup balsamic vinegar
1 to 2 cups chicken stock
1 tablespoon chopped herbs

Combine the mushrooms, shallots, onions, leeks, carrot, tomatoes and olive oil in a large ovenproof skillet. Sauté lightly. Add the chicken, wine, vinegar, chicken stock and herbs. Cook slowly in the oven or on the stovetop for 1 to 1½ hours or until the chicken is cooked through.

Yield: 4 to 6 servings

Worden's

LITTLENECK CLAMS WITH PROSCIUTTO, ROASTED PEPPERS AND SHARP CHEDDAR CHEESE

12 littleneck clams
Worcestershire sauce to taste
Tabasco sauce to taste
Bread crumbs as needed
12 small pieces roasted peppers
4 thin slices prosciutto, cut into thirds
4 thin slices sharp Vermont Cheddar cheese, cut into thirds

Scrub and shuck the clams. Season the clams with the Worcestershire sauce, Tabasco sauce and bread crumbs. Top each clam with 1 piece pepper, 1 piece ham and 1 piece cheese. Place in a baking pan. Bake at 350 degrees for 10 to 15 minutes or until the clams are cooked through.

Yield: 4 servings

Worden's

INDIAN PUDDING

2 quarts whole milk
1 cup Gray's white cornmeal
4 eggs, beaten
1½ cups molasses
1 teaspoon ginger
1 teaspoon nutmeg
½ teaspoon cinnamon
1 teaspoon vanilla extract
6 tablespoons unsalted butter

Heat the milk in a saucepan to 180 to 190 degrees. Add the cornmeal. Bring to a slow boil, stirring occasionally. Cook for 3 to 4 minutes, stirring occasionally. Add the eggs, molasses, ginger, nutmeg, cinnamon, vanilla and butter. Cook until heated through, stirring until blended. Pour into a greased 6x9-inch glass baking dish. Bake at 325 degrees for 1½ hours or until set. Serve with coffee ice cream.

Yield: 10 to 12 servings

Worden's

Index

Order Forms

Flavors from the SouthCoast

Coastline Elderly Services, Inc.
1646 Purchase Street
New Bedford, Massachusetts 02740
(508) 999-6400

Please send _____ copies of *Flavors from the SouthCoast*

@ $14.95 each $_____

plus postage and handling @ $ 3.50 each $_____

Total $_____

Name _____

Address _____

City _____ State _____ Zip _____

Please make checks payable to Coastline Elderly Services, Inc.

Flavors from the SouthCoast

Coastline Elderly Services, Inc.
1646 Purchase Street
New Bedford, Massachusetts 02740
(508) 999-6400

Please send _____ copies of *Flavors from the SouthCoast*

@ $14.95 each $_____

plus postage and handling @ $ 3.50 each $_____

Total $_____

Name _____

Address _____

City _____ State _____ Zip _____

Please make checks payable to Coastline Elderly Services, Inc.